FUN FOOD GOURMET GAMES

Susan Crook
Johnny McCune

with photography by
Katrina Lithgow

Kyle Cathie Limited

IN MEMORY OF JACK CROOK, BUNNY McCUNE
AND EMMA McCUNE

AND FOR MAGGIE, ENID, DICK, JENNY,
YO, ALEX AND HUGH – WITH LOVE

author biographies

Susan Crook and Johny McCune have a wide range of writing experience. Susan Crook is a former magazine journalist and author of *A Survival Guide to the Student Kitchen*. Johnny McCune used to work on the Big Breakfast (as on-screen games master for Chris Evans) and now works as Features Producer at GMTV. He is billed as the 'best games player anyone has ever met'

This edition first published in Great Britain 1999 by
Kyle Cathie Limited
20 Vauxhall Bridge Road
London SW1V 2SA

1 3 5 7 9 10 8 6 4 2

ISBN 1 85626 329 0

Designed by Button Design
Editor Kate Oldfield
Copy edited by Morag Lyle

A Cataloguing In Publication record for this title is available from the British Library.

Printed and bound in Singapore by Tien Wah Press Pte Ltd

CONTENTS

THE INTRODUCTION

This book is the perfect recipe for a dinner party that everyone will say is the best they've been to for ages. It serves up all the ingredients of great entertaining – good food, a great atmosphere and a hassle-free host or hostess.

the food and games

The majority of the menus comprise three courses and each course is followed by a game. The games range from brain-teasing icebreakers after the starter through to post-prandial raunchy contact sports that will have everyone blushing the next day!

The food is stylish, delicious and foolproof. You can get all the ingredients in a large supermarket, so no specialist shopping. We talk you through every stage of every recipe and game so you know exactly what to do when. No more frantic activity in the kitchen while your guests have fun elsewhere – with a bit of preparation you can have as much of a laugh as they do. And if you do need to get back to the kitchen you can leave your guests playing a carefully explained game while you add the finishing touches to the next mouth-watering course.

All recipes serve 8. Divide and multiply according to the number of guests you've invited. Ditto for the games.

the planning

Obviously your time's your own, but for the main dinner parties we've worked on a very basic – and very flexible – chronology of:

* Invite your guests for 8.00
* When they turn up at 8.20 – give them a drink

* Serve the starter at 8.45
* Play a game until 9.30, then serve the main course
* Play a game from 10.00 to 10.30 then serve pudding
* Start the last game at 10.45.

top tips!

We've done a fair few dinner parties in our time, so here are our top 12 tips which you might find useful as you get into this book:

1 It should look effortless to your guests, but a good dinner party does require effort on your part. Allow yourself time to shop and prepare ahead where necessary. Don't panic – no one will starve if things go wrong and the games are there to give you a breather.

2 Before you start inviting the world and his wife round to be impressed by your new-found entertaining skills, make sure you have the right equipment. Don't, for example, invite 10 people for dinner if you've only got 7 chairs and 6 knives. Buy, beg or borrow.

3 Similarly, consider your crockery. Don't do soup and ice cream in the same meal if you've only got 8 bowls (unless you actively enjoy washing up in the middle of a dinner party). All the recipes in this book have been carefully planned to avoid this. While we're on the topic of crockery, and if you happen to be buying, don't just look at plates: consider large soup or pasta bowls for main courses too.

4 A few other bits of basic kit in your kitchen will make sure that your cooking is even more polished. Make sure that you have a pastry

THE INTRODUCTION CONT...

brush, a flat baking tray and a food processor.

3 The most important piece of equipment you need is a constantly boiling kettle. Don't even think about tackling these recipes unless you've got an electric kettle that switches itself off when it's done. There's nothing worse than thinking that all you've got to do before you dish up is quickly boil the vegetables and then have to wait 5 minutes for the water to heat up.

4 Certain basic grocery items are used again and again in this book, so it's worth keeping your store cupboard topped up with quality olive oil, cooking oil, salt, black pepper, good stock cubes, chilli sauce and soy sauce. And always make sure you've got lots of ice cubes for drinks, games and morning-after ice packs...

7 Your life will be a lot easier if you can learn to think like a TV chef; an horrendous idea we know, but you'll notice they have everything they need close at hand and ready to use. So if you need to stir something in at the last minute, try to have it ready peeled, chopped or whatever it needs and placed near the cooker.

8 This book aims to get you out of the kitchen as much as possible, but don't have so much fun you forget that you are cooking – those oven timers that bleep at you are a godsend.

9 Quantities of salt and pepper aren't specified in the recipes so when they're ready – taste, season and taste again.

10 Although most guests will bring a bottle or two,

there's nothing worse than running out, so have a couple of white and red by you. Keep the white in the fridge so the warm plonk your guests bring has a chance to chill.

11 All the equipment for the games in this book can be found around the house, although it might be worth stocking up on string, playing cards, candles and breath freshener for all the snogging games!

12 Have a cab number handy – at some point you'll want your guests to go home.

here's how to get around...

We have used the following symbols throughout the shopping lists and methods so that you know which course we are referring to (and to help you if you want to miss out certain courses from a party menu).

- S **starter**
- M **main course**
- P **pudding**

We have also flagged certain games which might shock your more sensitive guests (such as your granny, the vicar or your boss). Look out for the following symbols and replace the games, if needs be, with a more appropriate – and genteel – one from another party menu.

- ! **flesh games**
- X **granny unfriendly**
- ☺ **good, clean family fun**

VAGUELY SUMMERY

in which our friends break the ice...

The dinner party starts innocently enough but can finish with guests getting very intimate indeed. Inbetween there are buttock muscles to be flexed and a delicious summery menu to enjoy. This is a meal that proves you really may not be able to make an omelette without breaking eggs...

THE MENU

BAKED PEPPERS AND MOZZARELLA

the egg trick

ORIENTAL SALMON WITH
STIR FRY NOODLES

the tupenny game

CHOCOFFI ICE-CREAM

the credit card game

Bunty began to feel curiously nervous about Freddie's intentions…

THE SHOPPING

S baked peppers

4 large red peppers
(try to get roundish ones rather than long thin ones)
4 fresh plum tomatoes
8 teaspoons tomato pesto
(or plain, if you prefer)
olive oil
200g (7oz) mozzarella
fresh basil
2 tablespoons balsamic vinegar
200g (7oz) mixed salad leaves
loaf of good bread & butter

M oriental salmon

8 thick salmon fillets
(about 1.5kg or 3lb in total)
2 teaspoons ready chopped ginger paste
2 teaspoons Chinese five-spice powder
2 cloves garlic
6 tablespoons soy sauce
2 teaspoons chilli sauce
(or 1 teaspoon chilli powder)
2 tablespoons cooking oil
1 tablespoon sesame oil
6 courgettes
6 carrots
300g (11oz) mushrooms
small bunch fresh coriander
500g (1lb 2oz) medium egg noodles
NB: you'll need a pastry brush for this recipe

P chocoffi ice-cream

300g (11oz) dulce de leche
(Argentinian condensed milk – or make it yourself by chucking an unpierced 350g tin of condensed milk in a saucepan of boiling water for a couple of hours)
1 large tablespoon golden syrup
500g (1lb 2oz) mascarpone
100g (3½oz) plain yoghurt
6 plain chocolate digestives

the 'egg trick'

6 eggs
(and six more in case of breakages!)
6 small matchboxes, all identical in size
(also dig out a rolling pin, a baking tray – a good solid one with a tiny lip – and your least favourite tumblers!)

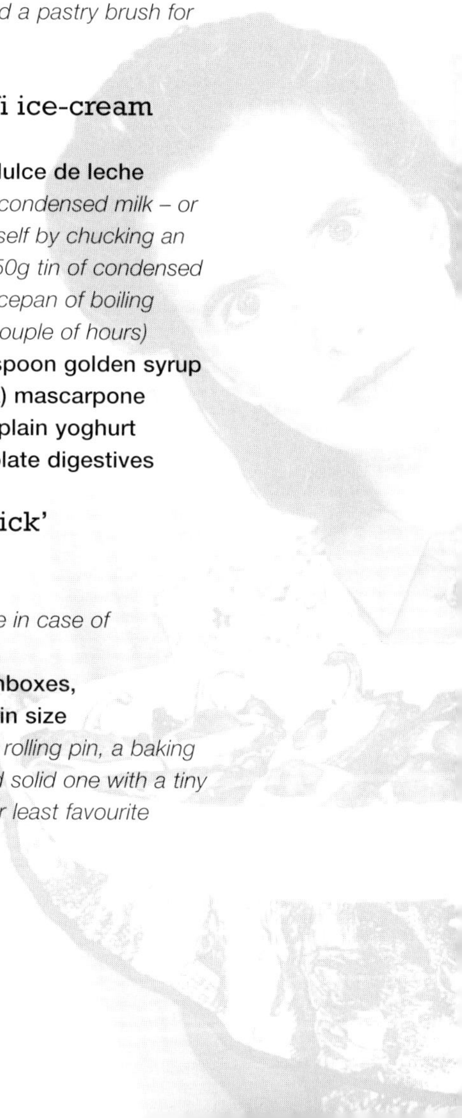

TO PREPARE THE MEAL

1 Make the ice-cream up to a week before or on the morning of the party. Put all ingredients, except biscuits, into a bowl and mix thoroughly (you could give it a brief whiz in a food processor). Put the biscuits in a freezer bag and knot it. Crush the biscuits to crumbs and stir in to the rest of the ingredients. Empty it all into a Tupperware or old ice-cream box. Cover and put in freezer.

2 Prepare the peppers. Pre-heat the oven to 180°C/350°F/gas mark 4. Cut the peppers in half lengthwise (leaving on the stalks) and remove the seeds and white pith. Roughly spread a teaspoon of pesto in the bottom of each pepper. Slice the tomatoes in half lengthwise too and fit into the peppers, cut side up. Slug a dash of olive oil on to each tomato and season well with salt and pepper. Put all the peppers into a roasting tray and roast for 20 minutes. When done, slice the mozzarella and layer on top of peppers. Leave to one side (they'll wait around quite happily for a few hours).

3 To prepare for the main course, mix the ginger, five-spice powder, crushed garlic, chilli and 4 tablespoons of the soy sauce. Wash and slice the mushrooms. Top, tail and peel the carrots, quarter lengthwise and cut into thin strips. Top and tail the courgettes and cut into thin strips too. Leave the veg in a bowl by the cooker. Put the noodles in a large saucepan and fill the kettle with water. Place the salmon on your grill pan, skin side up, and leave to one side. Pour the cooking oil (and sesame oil if using) in to a large frying pan or wok.

4 Put bread and butter on the table with appropriate knives. Don't martyr yourself with that 'part-cooked bread' stuff. You've got enough to do!

5 Prepare the equipment for the 'egg trick' but don't set it up yet – you don't want broken eggs all over the kitchen. As soon as your guests arrive, reheat the oven to 180°C/350°F/gas mark 4. Greet your chums and have a drink

THE MEAL CONT...

Ten minutes before you want to eat, pop the peppers back into the oven to melt the mozzarella (don't overcook or the cheese will turn to rubber). Arrange the salad leaves on the side of 8 small plates. In a processor (or with a fork), whiz together the balsamic vinegar and 2 tablespoons of olive oil with some torn basil leaves, salt and pepper.

Place a pepper on each plate and pour a little basil dressing onto the leaves. Before you sit down, turn the grill on high (making sure the salmon is well clear – you don't want to over-cook it) and leave the kettle to boil.
When everyone's finished the starter, get ready to amaze your guests with...

the egg trick (p16)

You'll need a clear 10 minutes to finish off the main course – plenty of time for your friends to create eggy mayhem.

meanwhile, back to the kitchen...

Boil the kettle and place the salmon under the grill for 4 minutes (don't forget about it!). Heat the oil in the pan and add the vegetables. Stir fry gently.

Pour hot water from the kettle over the noodles and cook according to instructions on the packet.

Turn the salmon over and brush with the soy mix before putting it back under the grill for another 4 minutes. Pour the rest of the soy mix over the veg with the remaining soy sauce and 2 tablespoons of water.

When the noodles are cooked, drain and add to the stir-fried veg.

Serve the salmon on to plates. Give the noodles a good stir, add a splash more water if it looks dry (you're aiming for everything to be well-coated, not dripping in sauce) and sprinkle over coriander leaves. Dish up and enjoy.

After the main course, pull the ice-cream out of the freezer to soften. Now it's time to digest and flex those buttocks...

the tupenny game (p16)

Play as long as you like, but bear in mind that the ice-cream needs about 15 minutes to soften. (Whack it back in the freezer if you're over-running and the competition is reaching a climax).

meanwhile, back to the kitchen...

Slip away to fill the kettle (for coffee) and serve up the ice-cream for pudding. It's VERY rich so don't over do it.

Accept compliments gracefully, whip out your credit card and pucker up. This is the point that your guests are grateful you haven't been over zealous with the garlic. Tonight could be someone's lucky night. Its time to play...

the credit card game (p17)

THE EGG TRICK

you will need

6 eggs
  (hardboiled if you prefer)
6 small matchboxes,
  all identical in size
6 cheap tumblers,
  each half full of water
a baking tray or a tea tray
a rolling pin or an empty wine
  bottle

aim of the game

To knock all 6 eggs, unbroken, into the glass tumblers.

how to do it

Place the 6 glasses of water on the table with the baking tray balanced on top. Remove insides of the matchboxes, take the outer section and squeeze shorter sides towards each other to create a shape round enough to hold an egg. Align the matchboxes on top of the tray immediately above the centre of each glass – THIS IS CRUCIAL. Place an egg on each matchbox. Deal the tray a short, sharp blow with the rolling pin. Hey presto, 6 floating eggs, one flying tray, 7 very impressed guests. Leave them to work it out and have a go themselves (you may need the other half dozen eggs!).

tips

Clear a path for the tray on the table to avoid broken wine glasses. Don't over fill tumblers. If you've just had your pad interior designed, hard boil the eggs!

THE TUPENNY GAME

you will need

Firm buttock muscles
A stack of two-pence pieces
  (get your guests to cough up, you've spent enough already)
A pint glass or empty jam
  jar *(an old mug would do)*

aim of the game

To walk a set distance carrying a stack of two-pence pieces clenched firmly between the

gluteus maximus and then deposit them safely into a waiting glass in a swift and inelegant move.

how to play

Decide on a start line – we use the edge of a rug, but a paper marker on the floor or a doorway will suffice. The number of coins attempted in one run is left to the players' discretion. Show offs who attempt to clench more than 10 will quickly learn the error of their ways! Set your guests off one after the other to attempt the course.

tips

Take your time and do it slowly. The best results are achieved with the knees together. Susan's biggest success was while wearing leather trousers! Tight skirts aren't recommended. Variations include walking backwards and setting a small assault course a cushion slalom, round the coffee table, over the dog – that kind of thing…

THE CREDIT CARD GAME

what you need

One credit card
A fine pair of lungs
Lucious lips

aim of the game

To pass the credit card from mouth to mouth using nothing but the suction power of your own lips.

how to play

Kick the game off yourself by tipping your head back and placing the credit card flat on your lips. Suck. Turn to person on your right, they will suck the card from your lips and pass it on to the person on their right. See how far you can get it round the table without someone dropping it and getting an unexpected full-on smacker.

tips

Don't suck too quickly or you'll run out of puff. Don't let go until you can feel that the next person has got their suction sussed. Don't spoil it for everyone else by deliberately just snogging.

A NO-MEAT MENU

in which the ibble was dibbled

Delicious enough for committed carnivores, here's a menu for veggie chums. The games are less kind to dumb animals – if your guests aren't on the ball they may end up with sore heads (and not just from the booze!). But at least they'll get a kiss out of it!

THE MENU

WALNUT, PEAR AND BLUE CHEESE SALAD WITH PEAR DRESSING

spoon tapping

SWEET POTATO CASSEROLE WITH SOBA NOODLES

ibble dibble

PLUM COMPOTE WITH SUMMER FRUIT GRANITA

train game

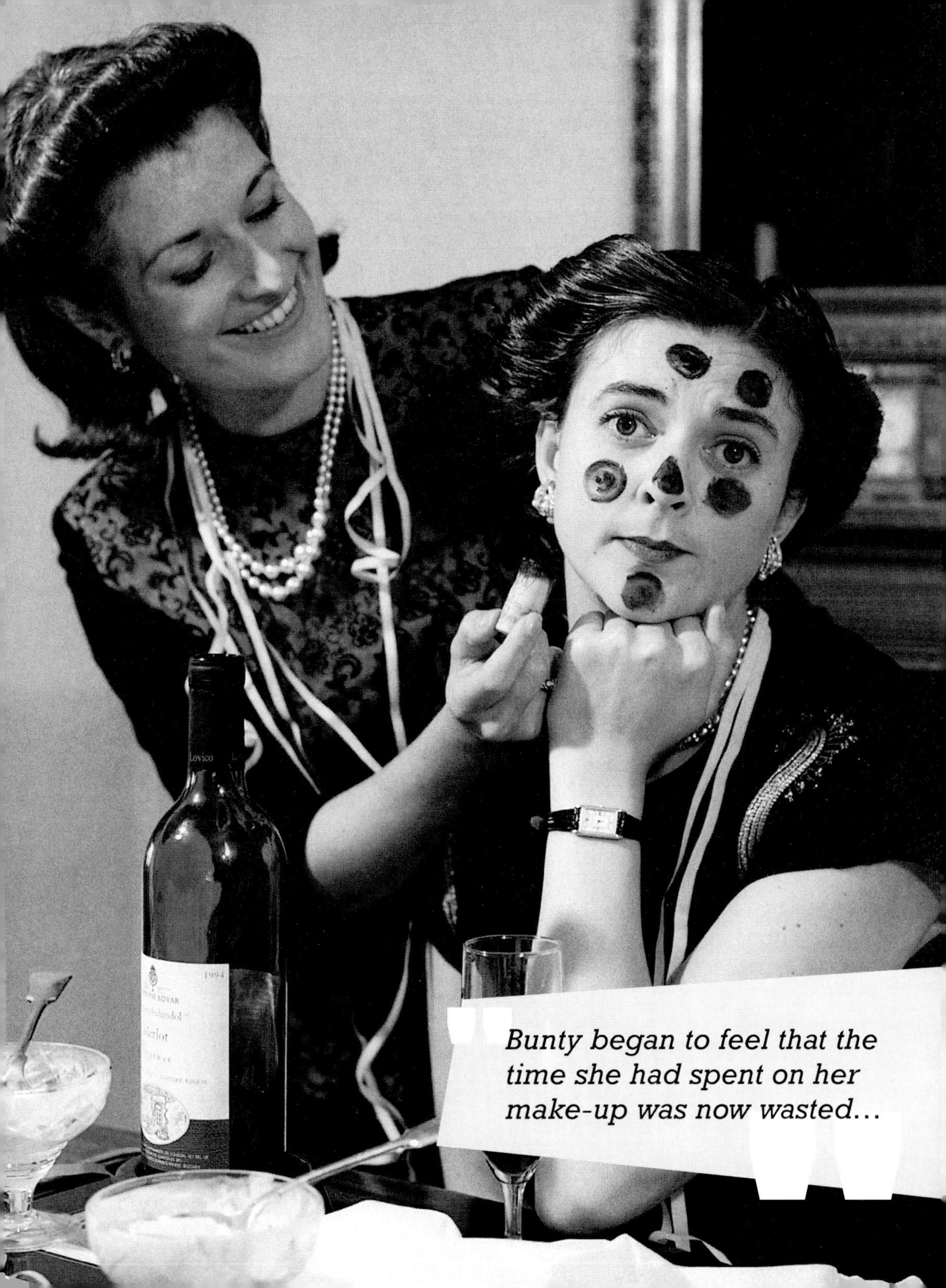

Bunty began to feel that the time she had spent on her make-up was now wasted…

THE SHOPPING

(S) the salad

400g (14oz) fine green beans
100g (3½oz) chopped walnuts
200g (7oz) Rocquefort cheese, cubed
4 ripe pears
2 tablespoons lemon juice
6 tablespoons walnut oil

(M) the casserole

cooking oil
2 onions, peeled and chopped
800g (1lb) sweet potato, peeled and cut into chunks
2 cloves of garlic, peeled and finely chopped
2 red peppers, de-seeded and chopped
1 red chilli, de-seeded and chopped
750ml (1¼ pint) vegetable stock (a cube is fine)
2 x 400g (14oz) tins of black-eyed beans
juice of 2 limes
500g (1lb 2oz) Soba (buckwheat) noodles
small pot of double cream
3 tablespoons chopped fresh mint

(P) plum compote

2 summer fruit tea bags
6 tablespoons sugar
1 bottle of dry red wine
3 star anise
1 red chilli
1 vanilla pod
1kg (2½lb) plums
250g (9oz) frozen raspberries

'ibble dibble'

Don't forget to get a candle or two for Ibble Dibble

TO PREPARE THE MEAL

1 Put the tea bags and 3 tablespoons of sugar in a freezer-proof container. Pour over 570ml (1 pint) of boiling water and stir until the sugar dissolves. Leave to stand until cold. Remove the tea bags and put in the freezer for at least 2 hours.

2 Put the red wine, the remaining sugar, the star anise, chilli and vanilla pod in a saucepan. Slowly bring to the boil, stirring so the sugar melts. Simmer for 20 minutes. Leave to cool and if you've got time, halve the plums and remove the stones. Put them in a serving bowl with the frozen raspberries. Allow the syrup to cool a bit more and pour over the fruit.

3 For the main course, heat 2 tablespoons of cooking oil in a large pan. Cook the onions gently in the oil for a couple of minutes. Add the sweet potato, garlic, red peppers and chilli. Cook for another couple of minutes, then add the stock. Simmer for 15-20 minutes until the potato is just soft, then take off the heat. Drain and rinse the beans and stir into the casserole with the lime juice. Leave until you're almost ready to serve (it will keep for 24 hours like this).

4 Just before your guests are due, cut the green beans into 5cm (2in) lengths and chuck into a saucepan of boiling water for about 3 minutes (you want them to be pretty crisp). Drain and let the cold tap run over them until they've cooled down. Arrange on 8 small plates, sprinkle over the walnuts and Rocquefort.

5 Greet your guests and have a drink. Five minutes before you want to serve the starter, disappear off into the kitchen and core 3 of the pears (no need to peel). Slice them thinly on to the starter plates. Peel, core and chop the remaining pear and chuck into the blender with the lemon juice, walnut oil and salt and pepper. Whizz until the dressing is lovely and thick. Pour over the prepared salad and serve – taking the spoons and tea towels you will need to play....

spoon tapping (p23)

THE MEAL CONT...

meanwhile, back to the kitchen...

Scarper to the kitchen when your cunning ruse is discovered and allow yourself about 5 minutes to cook the noodles.

1 Cook the noodles according to the instructions on the packet, but don't rinse them in cold water at the end. While they're cooking, add the cream and mint to the casserole and re-heat slowly. Divide the noodles between 8 plates or pasta bowls, if you have them) and slosh the hot casserole on top. After this course play...

ibble dibble (p24)

meanwhile, back to the kitchen...

It's really just a case of dishing up, but the granita needs a good bashing with a fork.

7 Mash the granita to give it a granulated texture (it's basically just flavoured ice crystals). Divide the plum mixture between 8 bowls (make sure you fish out the chilli, vanilla and star anise as you go) and sprinkle the granita on top. Enjoy! You'll need lots of energy to play...

the train game (p25)

SPOON TAPPING ☺

you will need

2 desert spoons
2 blindfolds *(tea towels will suffice)*

aim of the game

To cause unnecessary pain to one of your guests (the victim).

how to play

NB: This can only be played on someone who has never played it before.

Explain to 2 of your guests that the object of the game is to hit their opponent's head with the cupped end of a spoon, but that they can only hold it in their mouth. Tell them that the loser is the first one to admit defeat, through pain.

Demonstrate the technique so everyone can see that it's very difficult and there's no danger of anyone getting hurt. Blindfold the victim first, and before blindfolding their opponent explain – silently, obviously (unless the victim is so securely blindfolded they've gone deaf as well) – that you'll do the tapping for them! Now to the contest: let the 'victim' have first crack, when their opponent moves in for the kill you give the 'victim' a short sharp crack on the head. This will infuriate the victim who in turn will try harder on their next turn. This goes on until either the victim concedes defeat or the laughter from the other guests gives the game away.

tips

Don't vent any harboured hatred and hit the victim too hard.
It's best to pick a victim with a good sense of humour who isn't three times your size. This is also probably not a game to play with Granny if she's got false teeth – she may not enjoy the rest of the meal if they've gone flying...

THE IBBLE DIBBLE ☺

you will need

A cork and a candle

aim of the game

Not to get a black face

how to play

Prepare the cork for ibble-dibbling by burning one of the circular ends in the candle. When you've got a thick layer of soot at one end allow it to cool – you're not trying to brand anybody. Start by giving everyone their ibble-dibble reference: you are Ibble Dibble number 1 with no Ibble Dibbles; the person on your left is Ibble Dibble number 2 with no Ibble Dibbles and so on. The essential thing to grasp is that the term 'ibble dibble' refers both to the players and the mark made by the cork.

The object of the game is to pass 'the Call' from one player to another; if a player falters or calls incorrectly then they get dibbled, which means that they have the cork twisted on their face to create a perfect black mark. That player then has to refer to themself, and be referred to, as Ibble Dibble number x with one Ibble Dibble. They then start the call again until the next person falters or makes a mistake. A natural end to the game is when someone's face is unrecognizable! Eg. If number 1 has no cork marks, number 2 has three cork marks on their face and number 8 has 1, it will go like this: The Call: 'Ibble Dibble number 1 with no Ibble Dibbles calls Ibble Dibble number 8 with one ibble dibble.' The return: 'Ibble Dibble number 8 with one Ibble Dibble calls Ibble Dibble number 2 with three Ibble Dibbles,' and so on.

tips

No one can ask how many Ibble Dibbles they've got, or tell anyone else if asked – a good player should be able to keep count.
Recharge the cork as often as necessary.
Don't let people wash their faces before they go home.
Wash your face before bed!
If you are teetotal it won't be much fun and you won't have any corks!

THE TRAIN GAME

you will need

A room, or a corridor, with a door dividing it from the dining area

aim of the game

A guaranteed snog!

how to play

Run around the room in a train-like fashion, with added 'Ivor the Engine' sound effects. Single out one member of the opposite sex and leave the room with them, again in a train-like fashion (think of them as being a carriage to your engine!).

Once out of the room shut the door and shunt to a halt. Move in as if you're going to kiss your carriage, but actually give them a short sharp smack on the cheek – don't worry, it gets better.... Once the carriage is over the initial shock explain that they will return to the room and pick up another carriage, but this time when the train shunts to a halt behind the door the engine will kiss the first carriage. The first carriage then turns to the second carriage who obviously expects a good smacker – but gets a smack instead. This goes on until every one has had a slapping. The only person to miss out on a kiss is the poor person at the end (who presumably no one fancies).

tips

Don't hit too hard – you don't want to be accused of GBH.
Encourage partners not to choose each other.
Encourage potential partners to choose each other.
Remember you will have to kiss your 'carriage' 6 times, so it's probably not politic to choose your best friend's fiancé.

QUITE A QUICK ONE

in which the parfaits are perfect

This is a particularly quick menu to prepare, good for after work dinner parties. The games call for quick thinking too, whether it's testing the brain with some teasers or testing your reflexes in Sam's Hands

THE MENU

THAI CRAB DIP

brain teasers

CHICKEN AND CEPS WITH ROAST NEW POTATOES AND SPICED SPINACH

sam's hands

RASPBERRY AND ORANGE PARFAITS

real charades

George's brainteasers were always dashed difficult, but that didn't deter Lavinia...

THE SHOPPING

S thai crab dip

1 bunch of spring onions (about 100g or 3½oz)
510g (1lb 2oz) white crab meat *(that's 3 tins)*
2 tablespoons sesame oil
2 tablespoons chopped fresh coriander
2 tablespoons chopped fresh basil
1 tablespoon chilli sauce *(add more if you like it hot)*
4 tablespoons mayonnaise
2 green peppers
2 red peppers
a few carrots
2 bags of prawn crackers

M the chicken dish

olive oil
8 skinless chicken breasts
juice of 1 lemon
150ml (¼ pint) white wine
1kg (2¼lb) small new potatoes
2 tablespoons chopped fresh rosemary & a few sprigs
500g (1lb 2oz) spinach
50g (2oz) butter
400g (14oz) tinned chopped tomatoes
50g (2oz) ceps (dried wild mushrooms), reconstituted
2 tablespoons chopped flatleaf parsley
1 nutmeg clove

P the parfaits

500ml (18fl oz) whipping cream
200g (7oz) orange curd
250g (9oz) raspberries, drained if frozen or canned
2 tablespoons lemon juice

TO PREPARE THE MEAL

1 You can make the pudding the morning of (or even the night before if you're going to be really pushed for time); do it first anyway. Pour the cream into the blender and beat until stiff. Slowly amalgamate the orange curd, then the raspberries. Don't let the fruit get too pulped, just give it a quick pulse. Add the juice a little at a time – you probably won't need all of it as the mixture needs to be fairly firm. Spoon the mixture into a large bowl (or individual ramekins), cover with clingfilm and chill.

2 Slice the spring onions finely and drain the crab meat. In a large bowl mix all the ingredients for the starter, except the prawn crackers and veg. Add more mayonnaise if you think the mixture is too stiff, but it should be pretty chunky. Refrigerate until needed. Cut the peppers and carrots into batons and arrange on a couple of serving platters – one for each end of the table leaving room for the prawn crackers.

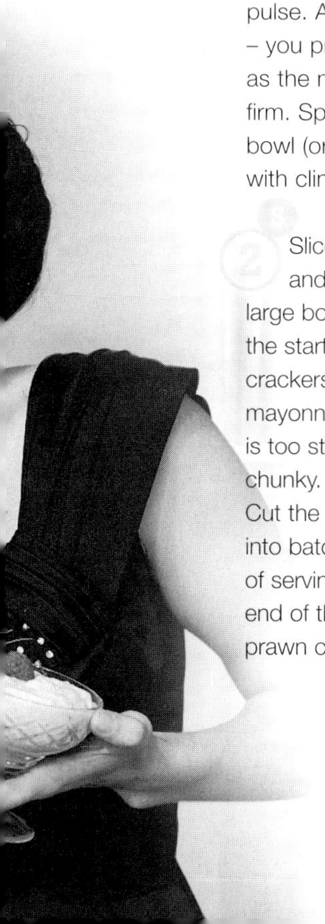

3 Heat 2 tablespoons of olive oil in a large casserole dish and brown the chicken. Add the lemon juice and wine. Boil for about 4 minutes, until the liquid starts to reduce. In the meantime, rinse the potatoes (cut them in half if they're too big – anything larger than a golf ball will take too long to cook). Put them in a roasting pan with a couple of tablespoons of olive oil, the rosemary sprigs, and lots of salt and pepper. Give it all a good mix around. Rinse the spinach and pack into a saucepan with the butter. (The moisture clinging to the leaves will be enough to cook it.)

4 Take the chicken off the heat and stir in the tomatoes. Cover. This can now sit around for a few minutes while you heat the oven and greet your guests.

5 When your guests are due, put the oven on at 170°C/325°F/gas mark 3. When they've arrived, put the potatoes in – they need about 45 minutes-1 hour. The chicken needs about 40 minutes, but it will sit around quite happily in the oven for up to an hour, so put it in soon after the potatoes.

THE MEAL CONT...

To serve the starter, empty the packets of prawn crackers on to the serving platters and take the crab dip out of the fridge. Simple, really. Before you leave the kitchen, stir the ceps and their soaking liquid into the chicken, and give the potatoes a good shake.

Let everyone dip into the crab mix with the crackers and crudités. Explain to your guests that you've chosen a fishy starter deliberately to help boost their brain power for a couple of:

brain teasers (p31)

meanwhile, back to the kitchen...

You'll only need about 5 minutes to get the main course on the table, so leave your guests debating the brain teasers and head back to the kitchen.

Give the chicken and potatoes a stir. Mix the rosemary and parsley into the chicken. Put the spinach on the hob on a medium heat. Allow the butter to melt and keep it moving while the spinach wilts (this will take less than 5 minutes). Grate about half the nutmeg clove over the spinach as it cooks. Dish up the chicken and potatoes on to individual plates while the spinach cooks; put the veg into a serving bowl.

While everyone digests, you can relax and play Sam's Hands – all you have to do to the pud is get it out of the fridge.

sam's hands (p31)

meanwhile, back to the kitchen

Leave your guests to get in a tangle and dish up something that's less complex – pudding. This might be a good time to check that your bedroom isn't strewn with dirty underwear, because after everyone's tucked in, prepare to have your house ransacked for

real charades (p32)

BRAIN TEASERS

you will need

Lateral thinking
1 piece of paper and a pen

aim of the game

For the guest to work out the answer to a given scenario – it's not easy until you know.

how to play

Everyone racks their brains to work out an answer to the following question: 'A man is pushing his car around a corner. He stops in front of a building and automatically knows he's bankrupt. Why?'

They can ask all the questions they like, but you can only answer 'yes' or 'no'.

Answer: 'He's playing Monopoly.'

People will be thrown by asking questions such as 'Has the car run out of petrol?', 'Is the building a bank?' etc., though they might get it when they learn that the car hasn't got an engine and that the building is plastic!

Another simple (but irritating) brain teaser involves writing down the following words:

WOOD
JOHN
HANTS

Ask your guests to work out this person's full name and where they live (town and county).

Answer: John Underwood, Andover, Hampshire!

tip

It can get frustrating for people to keep guessing, so give them a few hints.

SAM'S HANDS

you will need

8 pairs of hands
Co-ordination
Forfeit glass of alcohol

aim of the game

Not to get the forfeit unless you feel you haven't drunk enough already.

REAL CHARADES

how to do it

Get everyone to place their hands on the table with their right hand over the arm of the person on their right. You will now have the right hand of the person on your left and the left hand of the person on your right in front of you!

Start off the round by saying 'To my right' and tap your right hand. The hand on the right of yours, (which will belong to the person sitting two to your right), has to tap and then the hand on the right of them (which will belong to the person directly on your right) has to tap and so on. If someone double taps a hand then the round changes direction. Any faltering or miss tapping results in the forfeit glass!

tips

Don't take your eyes off the table as the game gets very fast.
The crucial thing to remember is that the tapping order doesn't relate to where people are sitting around the table – *hands* should tap in order, not people!

you will need

A home full of potential: people will be foraging through your wardrobes and cupboards for props.
A spare room out of earshot where one team can practise.

aim of the game

For each team to produce a mini play with the title of a film/book/TV show cryptically concealed within it.

how to play

Decide collectively on how many words, excluding small ones, a title should be (2 is usually a good ballpark figure as this means that each team will perform 3 acts: for example *Wind in the Willows*).
Divide the table into two teams.
Real Charades involves all the performers taking part in each act.
Talking, wearing costumes and using props are essential.
Using the above example a team would have to come up with 3 different acts. The first act has to include the word 'wind', the second

act 'willows' and the third 'Wind in the Willows'. It is up to each team to hatch a cunning plot to disguise the word in the middle of the act so that the other team doesn't guess which is the key word or phrase. Each team performs one act alternately.

Taking the above as an example for one team: ACT I: you could have a scene of people boarding an aeroplane with the pilot talking about weather conditions, wind speed etc. Alternatively it could be a flatulence drama, but the dialogue must include the word wind.

ACT II: a father explains to his family what a cricket bat and ball are made of (the word willow must be included).ACT III: returning books to a mobile library and taking new ones out (including the *Wind in the Willows*).

tips

Throw in red herrings – you could incorporate several other titles as you go along. You could also introduce forfeits if not enough props or costumes are used.

WINTERY AND WARMING

in which things begin to hot up

An evening that will bring a glow to everyone's cheeks – either blushing at some rather risqué consequences, warming the cockles with comforting nosh or sharing body warmth in *Piggy's Coming*...

THE MENU

CHICKEN LIVER AND CHORIZO SALAD

consequences

FISH AND POTATO CASSEROLE

piggy's coming

BRIOCHE AND LEMON BUTTER PUDDING

acting chinese whispers

"the risqué game of consequences seemed to keep Aunt Esme amused ..."

THE SHOPPING

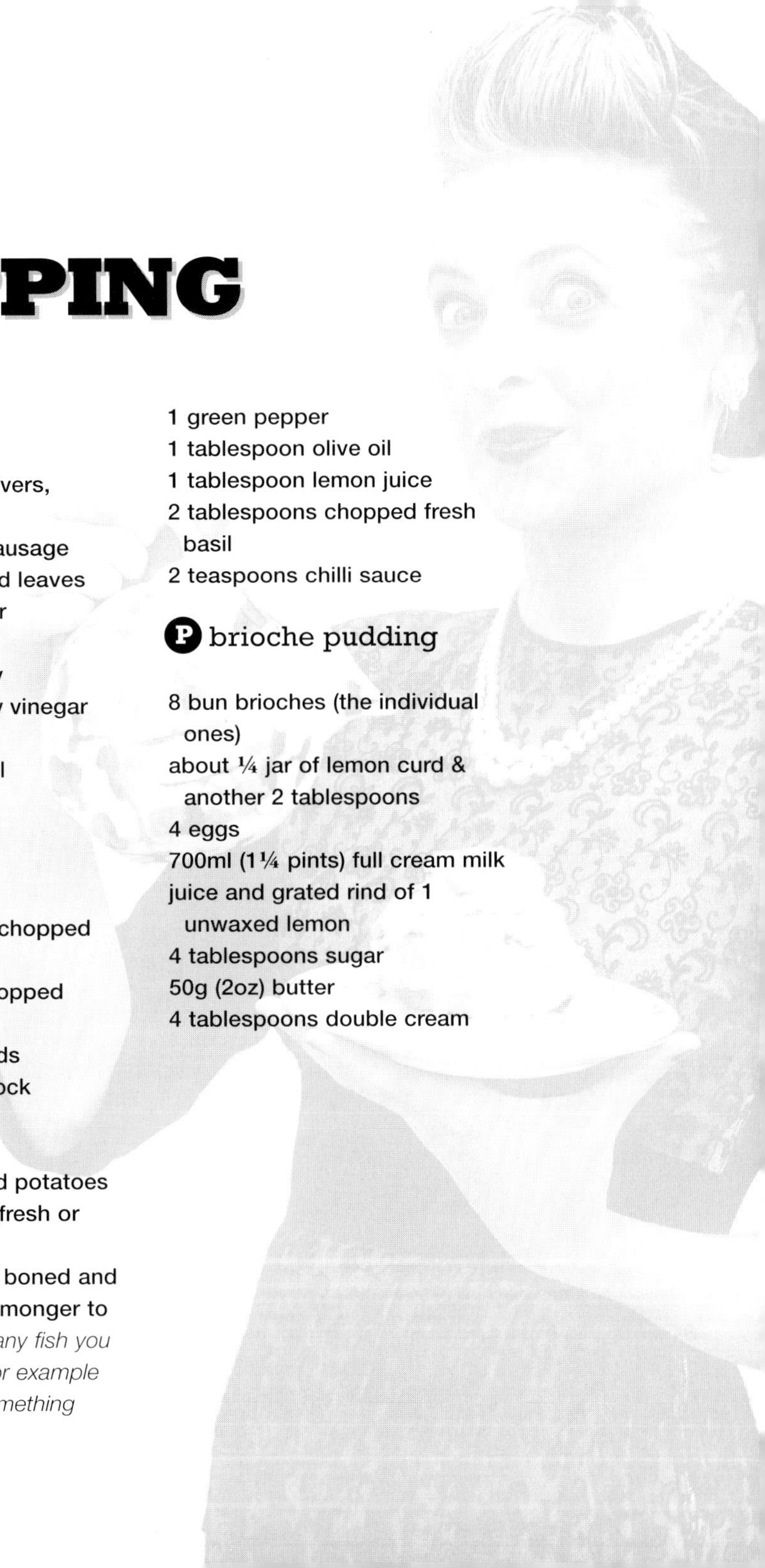

S the salad

600g (1¼lb) chicken livers, rinsed
300g (11oz) chorizo sausage
200g (7oz) mixed salad leaves
good bread and butter
cooking oil
120ml (4½fl oz) sherry
120ml (4½fl oz) sherry vinegar
1 teaspoon paprika
5 tablespoons olive oil

M the casserole

cooking oil
2 onions, peeled and chopped
4 leeks, sliced
400g (14oz) tinned chopped tomatoes
pinch of saffron strands
500ml (18fl oz) fish stock
1 glass white wine
2 bay leaves
1kg (2¼lb) small salad potatoes
100g (3½oz) prawns (fresh or frozen)
1kg (2¼lb) white fish, boned and skinned; get the fishmonger to do this for you *(use any fish you like – or a mixture – for example cod, haddock and something more exotic)*
1 green pepper
1 tablespoon olive oil
1 tablespoon lemon juice
2 tablespoons chopped fresh basil
2 teaspoons chilli sauce

P brioche pudding

8 bun brioches (the individual ones)
about ¼ jar of lemon curd & another 2 tablespoons
4 eggs
700ml (1¼ pints) full cream milk
juice and grated rind of 1 unwaxed lemon
4 tablespoons sugar
50g (2oz) butter
4 tablespoons double cream

TO PREPARE THE MEAL

1 To make the pudding, slice the brioches horizontally and spread one side of each slice with lemon curd. Layer all the pieces in a large ovenproof dish, making sure that you put the top crusts of the brioche on the top. Mix together the eggs, milk, grated lemon rind and 2 tablespoons of sugar. Pour over the brioche, making sure it gets a good soaking. Leave to stand.

2 While you're thinking pudding, prepare the sauce. Put 2 tablespoons of lemon curd, the lemon juice, 2 tablespoons of sugar and the butter in a small saucepan. Put it somewhere handy.

3 The first stage of the main course can be prepared well in advance. Heat 2 tablespoons of cooking oil in a large pan and gently cook the onions and leeks for about 5 minutes. Add the tomatoes, saffron, stock, wine and bay leaves. Bring to the boil and then simmer for 10 minutes. Cut the potatoes into thick slices and add. Cook for another 10 minutes. At this point you can switch the heat off and leave until you're almost ready to go.

4 Just before your guests are due, get the prawns out of the freezer (if necessary) and get the starter as ready as you can. Rinse the chicken livers and halve if they're huge. Cut the chorizo into thin slices. Arrange the salad leaves on 8 small plates. Put the bread and butter on the table.

5 Greet your guests and relax until 10 minutes before you want to serve the starter. Then head for the kitchen and fry the chorizo in 1 tablespoon of cooking oil until browned. Scoop out the sausage and leave to one side. Gently fry the chicken livers in the same oil for a couple of minutes. Mix in the sherry, olive oil, vinegar and paprika. Season well. Simmer for about 5 minutes until the livers are cooked and the liquid is syrupy. Stir the chorizo back in so it gets coated with sauce. Pop the oven on to heat at 170°C /325°F/gas mark 3 (for the pudding). Place the liver and chorizo mixture on top of the salad leaves and serve immediately. After this, get ready for…

consequences (p40)

THE MEAL CONT...

meanwhile, back to the kitchen...

Give yourself 10 minutes while your guests read out the consequences to get the fish cooked and served.

6 Head for the kitchen and start reheating the casserole base. Cut the white fish into chunks and add to the hot casserole. Cook for 5 minutes. While it's doing, chop the green pepper into small dice and mix with the olive oil, lemon juice, basil and chilli sauce. Add the prawns to the casserole and heat through. Serve into soup plates or pasta bowls with a dollop of the green pepper mixture on top of each serving.

7 Just before you leave the kitchen, whack the brioche pudding into the oven. It takes 45 minutes to cook, so bear that in mind while you're playing *Piggy's Coming*. If the game's over-running, switch the oven off and leave the pudding in there. It won't mind! Eat up now, because...

piggy's coming (p40)

meanwhile, back to the kitchen...

It will take around 5 minutes to heat the sauce and set out the brioche pudding artistically, so escape when you can.

8 Warm the sauce, stirring occasionally as the butter melts. In the meantime, get the pudding out of the oven and serve into bowls, making sure each one gets a brioche 'top'. When the sauce is hot and everything has melted, stir in the cream. Use a sharp knife to pierce each brioche top and pour in some of the sauce. Dribble the rest around each portion. Make sure there's an equal amount of sauce in each bowl and serve. Once everyone has had enough get ready to demonstrate your dramatic skills in...

acting chinese whispers (p41)

"Lavinia was very proud of her brioche pudding..."

CONSEQUENCES ☺

you will need

8 pens
8 pieces of paper
8 good imaginations

aim of the game

To write down the most bizarre coupling in the most obscure situations – don't worry, it comes naturally to most people. It may be an old game but it's much more fun playing as an adult.

how to do it

Get everyone to write down something for the first category from the list given, then fold the paper over to cover what's been written, and pass it on to the person on your left. In front of you, you now have a piece of paper with the top part folded over; write down a name from the next category, fold, and pass to your left. Carry on going through all 6 of the categories. Put all the folded pieces of paper into a bowl and shuffle them up; everybody then takes it in turns to pull one out and read the 'consequence'.

Categories
1. A man's name
2. A woman's name
3. Where they met
4. What he said to her
5. What she said to him
6. What the consequence was!

tip

It is always good to use the names of well-known people and places – or those well known to your guests. Guaranteed laughter!

PIGGY'S COMING ⓧ

you will need

7 chairs
Blindfold
Acute hearing

aim of the game

To identify the owner of the lap.

how to play

Get everyone to sit in a large circle, preferably on chairs. Choose one person to be blindfolded and place them in the middle of the circle. Spin the blinfolded person round at least 10 times – to make sure that they're completely disorientated. They then have to stagger from the centre of the circle and find a lap to sit on. Once seated, they must say 'squeal little piggy, squeal', to which the owner of the lap has to reply, in fluent pig language, with a short squeal. The blindfolded person has one guess as to the owner of the lap. If they call right then the 'piggy' becomes blindfolded, and the blindfolded becomes piggy. If wrong, it's back to the middle again.

tip

The larger the circle, the more fun you'll have.

ACTING CHINESE WHISPERS

you will need

A scenario

aim of the game

It's very similar to the verbal game where a sentence is whispered from one person to the next and by the time the time it's halfway round the table the sentence is completely different – you know the one. This has the same result, but is a little trickier.

how to do it

Send all your guests out of the room. Think of a scenario such as: a burglar breaking into an art gallery, bypassing the infra-red alarm beams and stealing an enormous picture – and write it down. Call in a guest and act it to them. They then call in someone else and act the scenario to them. And so on until everyone is back in the room. Having acted out the scenario to all the assembled guests, the last person has to explain what they think they've just acted. I guarantee it won't be anywhere near the original scenario you wrote down.

tip

Don't choose scenarios that are too long and complicated.

ONE TO PREPARE IN ADVANCE

in which you might lose your shirt

This is a great menu if you're going to have time to do some preparation the night before – on the day it's incredibly easy. It might be worth preparing what to wear too – as you may find youself stripping off…

THE MENU

CARROT AND FENNEL SOUP

scissors

ORIENTAL BAKED DUCK WITH BRAISED BOK CHOI

cahoots

MANGO AND COCONUT CRÉME BRÛLÉE

strip musical chairs

Johnny's legs made a rare and timid appearance in strip musical chairs.

THE SHOPPING

S the soup

50g (2oz) butter
2 onions, peeled and chopped
2 fennel bulbs, chopped
800g (1lb) carrots, topped, tailed and peeled
2 vegetable stock cubes
2 teaspoons chilli sauce
2 teaspoons ground coriander
juice of 1 lime
100ml (3½fl oz) thick natural yoghurt
chopped fresh coriander

M baked duck

8 duck breasts (skins on)
cooking oil
2 medium onions, peeled and chopped
4 cloves of garlic, peeled and crushed
2 tablespoons ready-mashed ginger paste
2 red chillis, seeded and finely chopped
150ml (¼ pint) mirin (or dry sherry & 2 tablespoons sugar)
150ml (¼ pint) white wine
2 tablespoons runny honey
6 tablespoons dark soy sauce
6 whole star anise
500g (1lb 2oz) mixed gourmet rice
800g (1lb) pak choi or 8 little gem lettuces
1 Thai or Chinese stock cube

P the brulées

600ml (1 pint) double cream
75g (3oz) creamed coconut *(the stuff in a block)*
3 star anise
3 large eggs
3 large egg yolks
2 tablespoons caster sugar
500g (1lb 2oz) drained, tinned mango slices – about 2 cans
4 tablespoons demerara sugar

There are a number of ways of achieving a hard sugar topping. If you have a blowtorch, use that. If not, stand the brûlée under a very hot grill when it comes out of the oven. And if you really can't be bothered, just sprinkle the sugar on top and hope that your guests are too polite (or too drunk) to comment. This isn't a classic brûlée recipe – a purist wouldn't include egg white – but it does have a lovely dense texture and will definitely set. If yours hasn't set in the allotted time, leave it in the oven till it does.

TO PREPARE THE MEAL

1 The day before, if possible, slash the skin of the duck breasts and place skin-side down in a dry frying pan. Cook over a low heat for 10 minutes, until the skin is browned and a lot of fat has been released. When it's done, throw the fat away and put the duck skin side-up in a large, ovenproof dish. Meanwhile, heat 1 tablespoon of oil in a pan and then gently cook the onion, garlic, ginger and chilli for 10 minutes. Add the mirin, wine, honey, soy and star anise and simmer for another 10 minutes. Pour it all over the duck and leave to marinate for as long as possible (up to 48 hours). When cool, put in the fridge and stir occassionally.

2 To make the brûlée, heat the cream with the creamed coconut and star anise until it almost boils. Stir to check the coconut has melted, take off the heat and leave to infuse for 10 minutes. Preheat the oven to 150°C/300°F/gas mark 2. Beat the eggs and yolks in a large bowl with the caster sugar until pale and fluffy. Take the star anise out of the cream and pour it over the egg mixture, stirring all the time.

3 Arrange the mango slices on the bottom of a large flat-ish dish (you want a large surface area) or 8 small ramekins. Mash the mango a bit. Pour the cream and egg mixture over the top. Stand the dishes in a roasting tin of hot water and bake for about 1 hour 10 minutes. Check it – the centre should be wobbly, but not liquid. Turn the grill up very high. Sprinkle the top of the brûlée with the demerara sugar and grill until it melts. Chill until needed.

4 The soup can be made the day before too, but it's quick to do on the night. Melt the butter in a large saucepan and gently cook the onion, fennel and carrots for about 10 minutes. Boil a kettle. Add the stock cubes, coriander and 2 litres (4 pints) of boiling water. Simmer for 30 minutes. Blend (in batches) and leave to one side until ready to reheat. (Actually, this is good if served very chilled on a hot day.)

5 Fifteen minutes before your guests are due, put the kettle on and measure the rice into a saucepan. Preheat the oven to

THE MEAL CONT..

180°C/350°F/gas mark 4 and take the duck out of the fridge. As you hear the doorbell ring, chuck the whole dish of duck and marinade into the oven. It will take around 1 hour 15 minutes to cook, or slightly less if you like your meat rare.

Five minutes before you want to serve the soup, stir in the lime juice and chilli sauce and bring it back to a simmer – don't let it boil. Halve the pak choi lengthwise and put in a lidded casserole dish with the stock cube. Refill the kettle and boil again.

Dish up, dolloping a spoonful of yoghurt on to each bowl of soup and sprinkling over some fresh coriander. Get someone else to carry the bowls through while you put some heat under the rice – if you start it off with cold water it should take about 40 minutes. Cover the pak choi in boiling water so the stock cube dissolves and put in the bottom of the oven. The veg will be happy in the oven for anything between 25 and 40 minutes. Grab a pair of scissors for the game.

scissors (p48)

meanwhile, back to the kitchen…

Once someone else has sussed the scissor game, you can leave them to adjudicate and slip back to the kitchen. You only need to dish up.

Serve the rice and duck plus sauce on to plates. Drain the pak choi and put in a serving dish. Hard work over. Time to get into…

cahoots (p48)

meanwhile, back to the kitchen…

Pull the brûlée(s) out of the fridge and serve.

After pudding, make sure you are wearing lots of layers because it is time to play…

strip musical chairs (p49)

Soup anyone?

SCISSORS ☺

you will need

1 pair of scissors
Flagon of wine for the forfeits

aim of the game

It's another lateral thinking game, but this time there are penalties to pay.

how to do it

Pass the scissors, opened or closed, to the person on your left and ask them, 'Are they crossed or uncrossed?' The recipient will obviously reply according to whether the scissors are open (crossed), or closed (uncrossed). Only you know that the correct answer depends on whether your legs are crossed or uncrossed, not on the position of the scissors. If a guest answers incorrectly they must pay a drinking forfeit. They then pass the scissors on and ask the same question. The correct answer always depends on the leg position of the person holding the scissors. Obviously you will have to adjudicate, so make sure you can see everyone's legs.

tip

Encourage people who guess what's going on not to give it away to the others.

CAHOOTS ☺

you will need

An accomplice *(with sharp hearing)*

aim of the game

To convince your guests that you and your accomplice are telepathic.

how to play

Tell your accomplice the game first. Explain to your guests that the telepathy between you and your accomplice is so strong that you can tell at whom they are pointing, even when you are outside the room. You will call, 'Are you in cahoots?' and they will respond, 'Yes, I'm in cahoots' while they point at someone. They must point at the last person to speak before you

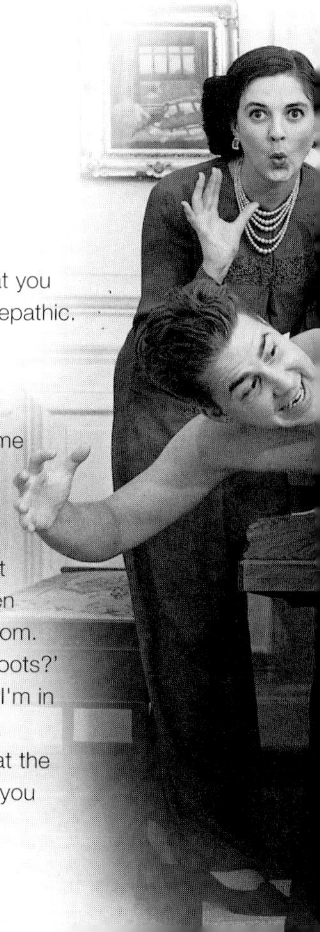

asked the question. They then ask 'Who am I pointing at?' Hopefully if you really are in cahoots you've got it right. Let your guests start talking among themselves before you ask the question.

tip

If there's more than one person talking your accomplice shouldn't be afraid to say that they're not in cahoots. You then start the call again.

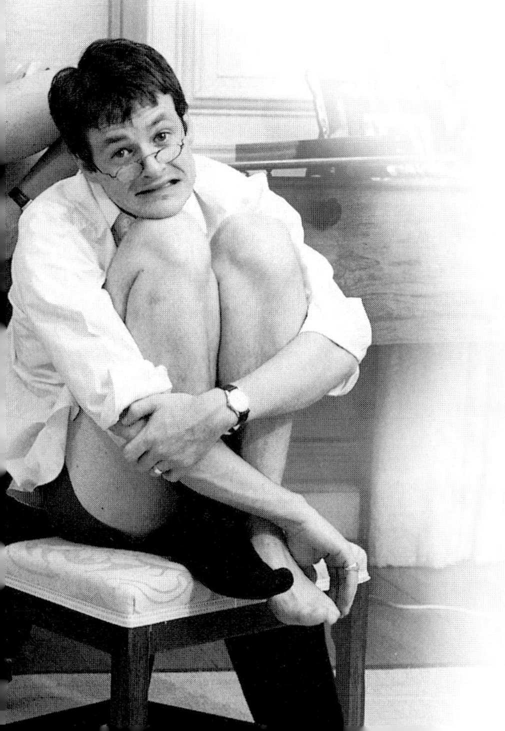

STRIP MUSICAL CHAIRS

you will need

Music
chairs

aim of the game

To sit on a chair when the music stops. (But you probably knew that already.)

how to play

Place the chairs (or you could use cushions) in the centre of the room. You need to man the music system. All the guests have to walk/dance round the chairs while the music is playing. When you switch the music off everyone has to try and sit down on one of the seats. There will be one guest who is too slow and will find that they haven't got a seat: they have to remove an item of clothing.

tips

Make sure that there is always one seat fewer than the number of people playing!
Have some upbeat music.
Wear lots!

VIBRANTLY VEGETARIAN

in which the cards come in handy

An evening designed for non-meat-eating smokers with eclectic tastes, good general knowledge and lightening reactions. That should cover just about everybody...

THE MENU

WILD MUSHROOMS WITH ROCKET AND PECORINO

penny and cigarette

THAI GREEN CURRY WITH JASMINE RICE

hat game

CINNAMON APPLE TART

hello jack

"Bunty didn't realise that you had to salute the King..."

THE SHOPPING

S wild mushrooms

400g (14oz) mixed wild mushrooms
400g (14oz) chestnut mushrooms
6 tablespoons olive oil
200g (7oz) rocket leaves
250g (9oz) young spinach leaves
chunk of pecorino cheese
4 tablespoons balsamic vinegar

M thai green curry

cooking oil
3-4 tablespoons Thai green curry paste
1 tablespoon fresh ginger paste
2 cloves of garlic, peeled and finely chopped
2 x 400ml (14fl oz) tins of coconut milk
2 aubergines, topped, tailed and cubed
4 red peppers, cores removed and chopped
2 large green mild chillis, de-seeded and chopped
400g (14oz) fine green beans, topped, tailed and halved
6 courgettes, topped tailed and sliced
500g (1lb 2oz) jasmine rice
4 kaffir lime leaves, chopped or grated rind of 1 lime
juice of 1 lime
2 tablespoons soy sauce
bunch of chopped fresh coriander

P apple tart

1 x 340g (12oz) slab of ready-to-roll puff pastry, defrosted if necessary
a bit of flour to roll the pastry out
50g (2oz) butter, melted
1 teaspoon ground cinnamon
500g (1lb 2oz) eating apples
2 tablespoons sultanas
3 tablespoons pine nuts
6 tablespoons demerara sugar
cinnamon ice cream or extra thick cream to serve

You'll need a pastry brush, a flat baking tray and a rolling pin for this recipe – no, it's not the egg trick again!

TO PREPARE THE MEAL

1 Roll the pastry out on a floured surface until it's almost as big as the baking tray. Brush the baking tray with some melted butter and slide the pastry on to it. Prick the surface of the pastry all over with a fork and put in the fridge for at least an hour.

2 Get all the veg ready. Heat 2 tablespoons of oil in a large saucepan and gently fry the two pastes for 30 seconds. Add the garlic and cook for another 30 seconds before adding the coconut milk. Chuck in the aubergine and peppers, cover and simmer for 10 minutes. Add chillis, beans and courgettes. Cook for another 5 minutes. At this point you can take it off the heat and leave to stand until you're nearly ready to serve.

3 If you get the chance before your guests arrive, wipe and slice the mushrooms. Mix the cinnamon into the remaining melted butter. You are now unbelievably prepared.

Five to 10 minutes before you want to serve the starter heat half the olive oil in a pan. Add the mushrooms and cook gently, stirring occasionally. Arrange the rocket and spinach on 8 small plates. Take a potato peeler to the pecorino and shave off long strips.

4 By the time you've done all this the mushrooms will be cooked. Stir in the balsamic vinegar

THE MEAL CONT...

and remaining olive oil and divide between the prepared plates of leaves. Sprinkle the cheese shaving on top and serve.

5 Clear the plates and head back to the kitchen. Put the kettle on and throw the rice in a saucepan. Collect the equipment you need for...

penny and cigarette (p55)

meanwhile, back to the kitchen...

The curry is virtually ready to go, but the rice takes 10 minutes and you need that time to get the pudding under way.

6 Cook the rice according to the packet). Gently reheat the curry and stir in the lime leaves or rind, juice, soy and chopped coriander.

7 For the pudding, core and thinly slice the apples (don't peel them). Arrange on top of the pastry so that they slightly overlap. (The fruit will shrink when cooked.) Sprinkle over sultanas and pine nuts, pushing them down among the slices of fruit. Brush with cinnamon butter and sprinkle the sugar on top.

8 Check the rice, drain and dish up with the curry. Don't leave the kitchen until you've put the oven on to heat to 200°C/400°F/gas mark 6 (for the pudding). Once everyone's finished eating, sling the tart in the oven and begin...

the hat game (p55)

meanwhile, back to the kitchen...

The tart takes 20-25 minutes to cook but it can be left to cool for a bit if you're on a winning streak.

9 Keep an eye on the pudding once it's been in the oven for 20 minutes – there's a fine line between golden brown and burned. Take it out and leave to cool for 10 minutes before cutting into slabs. Serve with cream or ice cream. Then clear the decks for:

hello jack (p56)

PENNY AND CIGARETTE

you will need

A pint glass
Piece of tissue paper, or loo roll
Rubber band or string
A 5p piece *(that's inflation for you)*
A cigarette *(If you're not a smoker there's bound to be one among your guests. If not, encourage someone to take it up or dust down the joss sticks)*

aim of the game

Not to be the one to let the coin drop into the pint glass.

how to play

Secure the tissue paper over the top of the pint glass – keep it quite taut and secure with an elastic band or string. Place the 5p piece in the centre of the tissue. Decide on a forfeit at the start of the game, for the person who causes the penny to drop into the glass. Each person then has to singe a part of the tissue using the lighted end of the cigarette without dislodging the penny. It gets more difficult the more goes you have!

tips

Each turn lasts until the edge of the hole just made stops burning. Make sure that there are no through draughts when it's your go!

THE HAT GAME

what you need

8 pieces of A4 paper
8 pens
A hat *(a bowl will suffice)*
A watch with a second hand

aim of the game

To describe as many of the names that your team pulls from the hat in one minute, as possible.

how to play

Divide your guests into 2 teams. Each person is given a sheet of paper which they then need to tear into 16 pieces. Write the name of well-known (to you all) or famous people on each piece. Fold and

THE GAMES CONT...

place in the hat. Decide which team is to go first. The first member has one minute to describe as many of the names they pluck from the hat as they can; you can only pull out another name after getting the first one correct. Unfortunately you cannot use key words when describing the person. For example if you were doing Tony Blair you can say, 'He's married to Cherie Booth,' but you can't say, 'He's married to Cherie Blair.' (Although if you had any brain at all you'd just say, 'He's Prime Minister' – but you get the idea.) A player can't put a name back in the hat if they get stuck. The winning team is the one who guesses most names correctly – so keep an eye on all these bits of paper, you'll need to count them!

tips

Don't pick names that are too obscure – you may know the name of the reserve goalkeeper in the 1954 Brazilian World Cup Squad but it's unlikely that anyone else will.

Don't let the timekeeper cheat.

HELLO ☺ JACK

you will need

One or more packs of cards *(it doesn't matter if they are not full sets)*

aim of the game

To lose all the cards in your hand.

how to play

Deal out all the cards face down. It is imperative that no one sees which cards they've been dealt. Starting from the dealer's left each player turns over one card and places it face up in the middle of the table. If a Jack is turned over everyone must shout 'Hello Jack'; if it's a Queen then everyone shouts 'Morning Queen'; if it's a King everyone salutes him with their right hand; and if it's an Ace then everyone slams their hand down on the pile. In all these instances the person who reacts last has to pick up the pile of cards from the middle of the table and add them to the bottom of their hand. The winner is the person who manages to lose all their cards. NB: when a player has just one card left they must let all the other players know by knocking on the table three times.

tip

It gets very loud and noisy, so delegate an umpire (yourself) – and your decision is final.

RATHER LOW ON WASHING UP

in which our friends lose the thread

If you're watching the pennies this probably isn't the menu to choose – large fresh prawns don't come cheap (but they do taste good). You'll need a 20cm (8in) cake tin with a removable base and greaseproof paper for this recipe. Don't be put off by the idea of baking – it's incredibly easy.

THE MENU

TANDOORI PRAWNS WITH MANGO SALSA AND NAAN BREAD

analogies

PORK WITH CUMIN, BLACK OLIVE MASH AND RED CABBAGE

fuzzy duck

MOCCA MELT

string game

In the string game it became obvious that Freddie and Roger both had a secret agenda...

THE SHOPPING

S the prawns

300ml (½ pint) natural yoghurt
juice of 1 lemon
1 small onion, peeled and finely chopped
2 cloves of garlic, peeled and chopped
1 tablespoon ginger paste
1 teaspoon chilli sauce
2 teaspoons garam masala
1 teaspoon paprika
800g (1lb) large raw prawns, heads and shells removed
1 large ripe mango
1 red onion
4 tablespoons chopped fresh coriander
2 tablespoons olive oil
8 mini naan breads

M pork with cumin

400g (14oz) button onions, or shallots
cooking oil
1kg (2¼lb) lean pork, cubed
1 tablespoon ground cumin
4 cloves of garlic, peeled and crushed
2 bay leaves
juice and grated rind of 1 lemon
400ml (14fl oz) white wine
1kg (2¼lb) red cabbage
2 cooking apples, cored and sliced
2 tablespoons sugar
1 tablespoon caraway seeds (optional)
300g (11oz) pitted black olives
1kg (2¼lb) potatoes
3-4 tablespoons olive oil

P mocca melt

250g (9oz) dark chocolate (with 70% cocoa solids)
4 tablespoons caster sugar
125g (4½oz) unsalted butter
100g (3½oz) ground almonds
1 tablespoon instant coffee dissolved in 2 tablespoons boiling water
4 eggs
250g (9oz) créme fraîche

TO PREPARE THE MEAL

1 Put the keys for the string game in the freezer. Peel the button onions. Heat 2 tablespoons of oil in a large pan and gently fry the meat until it browns. Add the onions and cook for 5 minutes more. Take off the heat and stir in the cumin, garlic, bay leaves, lemon and half the wine. Leave to one side until your guests pitch up.

2 To make the pudding, put all the ingredients except the eggs and créme fraïche in a saucepan and melt over the lowest possible heat, stirring occasionally. While this is going, on line the bottom of the cake tin with a circle of greaseproof paper (or silver foil, at a pinch). Oil the lined base and sides and then sprinkle a tablespoon or so of flour on top. Shake the tin to spread the flour around. Separate the eggs. Take the chocolate mix off the heat and stir in the egg yolks. If you've got to this stage and there's still a while to go before your guests arrive, stop here.

3 For the starter, mix together the yoghurt, lemon juice, onion, garlic, ginger, chilli, garam masala and paprika in a large pan. Stir in the prawns. Make the salsa by peeling and chopping the mango and red onion finely and stirring in the coriander and olive oil. Refrigerate until needed.

4 Cut the red cabbage into quarters, hack out the stalk and shred the rest. Put in a dish with the apples, the rest of the wine, 100ml (3½ fl oz) water, the sugar and caraway seeds (if using). Cover.

5 Fifteen minutes before your guests are due, preheat the oven to 180°C/350°F/gas mark 4. Beat the egg whites until very stiff. Carefully fold the whites into the chocolate mixture with a metal spoon. Pour into the cake tin. Put the casserole, cake and red cabbage in the oven (casserole at the top, cabbage at the bottom) when you hear the doorbell. The cabbage and casserole take about an hour, the cake 35 minutes. (The cake is lovely hot, warm or cold. I'm aiming for warm here, but if you're running late cook it while you're eating the first two courses and eat hot, or if you want to get the cooking out of the way, cook it earlier – even the day before.)

THE MEAL CONT...

6 Give yourself about 10 minutes in the kitchen before you serve the starter. As soon as you get to the kitchen, test the cake with a knife (if it comes out clean it's done) and take it out of the oven. Stir two thirds of the olives into the casserole.

7 Rinse the potatoes and chop into large chunks, removing any eyes or manky bits as you go. (Don't peel: better for you with the skins on.) Cover with cold water and put a very low heat under them. They'll take about 40 minutes to cook like this.

8 Gently cook the prawns in their yoghurty marinade. Make sure you cook them all on both sides. Chuck the naan in the bottom of the oven to warm through. Serve everyone a naan, some prawns in yoghurty sauce and a dollop of salsa on a large plate.

9 Get everyone to use the naan as a dishcloth – they'll need to keep their plates for the main course. (Saves on washing up.) Sharpen your wits and get ready to play...

analogies (p63)

meanwhile, back to the kitchen...

Just a couple of minutes to get the potatoes mashed.

10 Chop the remaining olives. Drain the potatoes and mash with lots of salt and pepper, the olive oil and olives. The potatoes, casserole and red cabbage can all be dished up at the table – the plates are already there. After you have eaten, you can relax and play...

fuzzy duck (p63)

meanwhile, back to the kitchen...

Cut the melt cake into thin slices (it's very rich) and serve with a blob of créme fraîche on the side. After this, it's time for...

string game (p64)

ANALOGIES ☺

you will need

An enquiring and creative mind

aim of the game

To describe a famous person or someone well known to everyone around the table in analogies.

how to play

The person sitting to your left thinks of someone well-known. Everyone else asks, in turn, for an analogy about that well-known person. For example, 'If the person were a car what type would they be?' (Other categories could be flowers, trees, TV programmes etc.). Each person is allowed one guess after their question's been answered. If they are correct then it's their turn to think of a well-known person.
NB: if choosing people known to your guests, or even people sitting around the table, it can get quite heated!

tips

Explain to the other players that the categories they use to describe the person shouldn't be the one they think is that person's favourite, but the one that is most similar to their personality. Make things easier to begin with by choosing a category like living people, famous sportsmen, TV personalities etc.

FUZZY DUCK ⊗

you will need

Nothing but a sharp mind and a clear head – although it may be a bit late in the evening for that.

aim of the game

To pass on the call 'Fuzy Duck' or 'Ducky Fuzz' without making an error. (Basically it's a way of getting people to say rude words.)

how to play

Say the phrase 'Fuzzy Duck' to the person on your left. They then repeat the phrase to the person on their left etc. If someone says 'Does

FUZZY DUCK CONT...

he?' (and anyone can say that, whenever they want) then the call changes direction and become 'Ducky Fuzz' as it goes round to the right until someone else says 'Does he?' This is the cue to revert to the original direction and call. Each time someone either falters or gets their words out incorrectly give them a forfeit or make them drink. NB: don't let two people say 'Does he?' consecutively or it could get rather boring for everyone else.

tips

Play it fast and loose.
Don't play this with your granny (unless she's very liberal!).

THE STRING GAME X

you will need

2 long pieces of string
2 keys *(it's best if they have been chilled in the freezer for a while – so get them out now.)*

aim of the game

To pass a key, which is attached to a piece of string, up or down the clothing of all the players so that they are joined together and then tie the end of the string to the beginning, creating a circle. (This game can be played as a race around the table or standing in the middle of the room)

how to play

Divide your guests into 2 teams. For each team, cut a length of string, approximately as long as the combined height of the team minus a third. (About 4-5 metres or yards in total.) This is a flesh game too. The object is for the first team member to pass the string up the clothing of the next (the threadee is not allowed to help the threader). When this feat has been accomplished successfully then the threadee now becomes the threader and has to pass the cold key down the clothes of the next team member. The winning team is the one that is completely threaded, with the 2 ends knotted together, first.

THE STRING GAME CONT...

tips

Don't cut the string too long as it's more fun if the teams have to huddle up close to one another.
The further you are from the beginning, the warmer the key will be.
The first person shouldn't let go of their end of the string – it may never be seen again.
Remember that the person having the key threaded through them is not at liberty to help.
It's quickest to thread up a player if they're standing on their head – use a wall to lean on or pick the yoga fans for your team.

INSPIRINGLY GLOBAL

in which we prove we've travelled

Time to show that you're a man or woman of the world with an internationally-inspired menu and some games that are definitely for adults only!

THE MENU

SAAG BHAJI SOUP WITH POPADUMS

sperm whale

LAMB TAGINE WITH COUSCOUS

association

AMARETTI AND CALVADOS TART WITH BAKED APPLE

lips united

Freddie hoped madly that Helga would be next in line...

THE SHOPPING

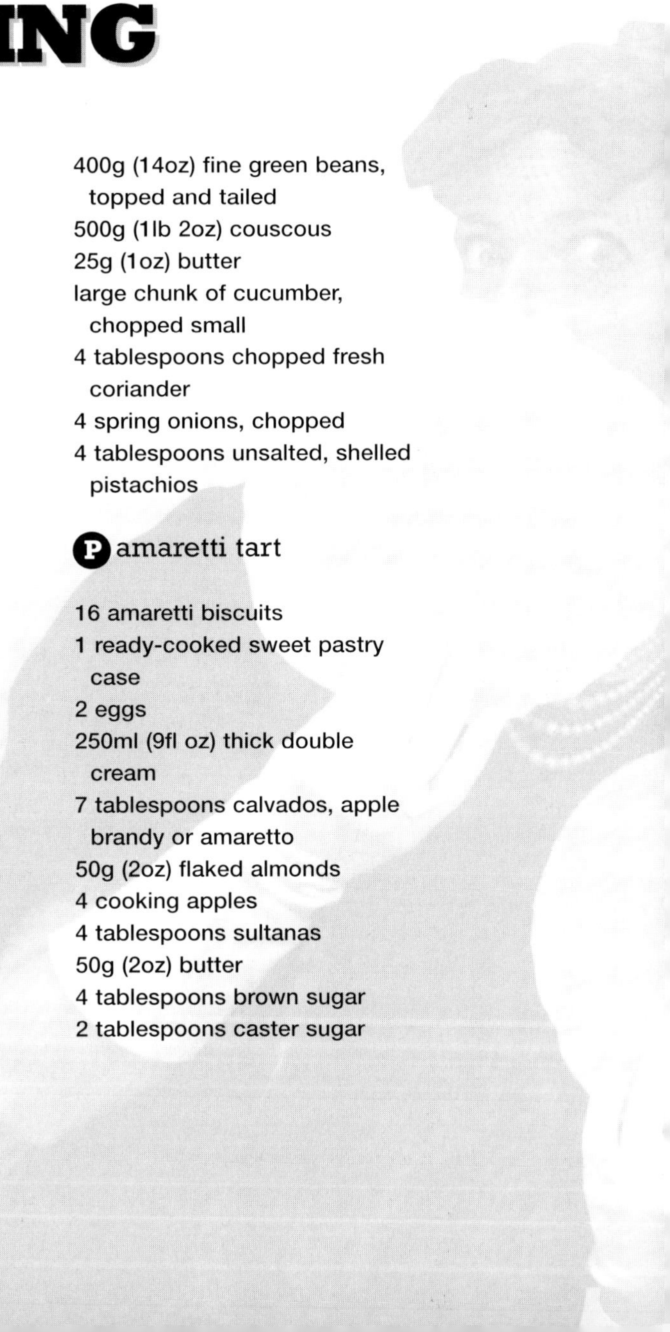

S the soup

50g (2oz) butter
4 tomatoes, roughly chopped
2 onions, peeled and chopped
1 green chilli, de-seeded and chopped
2 cloves of garlic, peeled
2 teaspoons ginger paste
500g (1lb 2oz) spinach
1 veg stock cube
16 popadums
½ jar of mango chutney
4 teaspoons garam masala

M lamb tagine

cooking oil
1kg (2¼lb) cubed lamb fillet
3 onions, peeled and sliced
1 teaspoon ground ginger
1 teaspoon chilli powder
1 teaspoon paprika
1 teaspoon ground cinnamon
1 tablespoon flour
2 cloves of garlic, peeled and crushed
400g (14oz) tinned chopped tomatoes
1 veg stock cube
2 tablespoons sultanas
400g (14oz) fine green beans, topped and tailed
500g (1lb 2oz) couscous
25g (1oz) butter
large chunk of cucumber, chopped small
4 tablespoons chopped fresh coriander
4 spring onions, chopped
4 tablespoons unsalted, shelled pistachios

P amaretti tart

16 amaretti biscuits
1 ready-cooked sweet pastry case
2 eggs
250ml (9fl oz) thick double cream
7 tablespoons calvados, apple brandy or amaretto
50g (2oz) flaked almonds
4 cooking apples
4 tablespoons sultanas
50g (2oz) butter
4 tablespoons brown sugar
2 tablespoons caster sugar

TO PREPARE THE MEAL

1 To make the soup, melt the butter in a large saucepan and add the tomatoes and onions. Cook for 5 minutes then stir in the chilli, garam masala, garlic and ginger paste. Rinse the spinach. Pack the veg into the saucepan and let it wilt down before adding the stock cube and 1.2 litres (2 pints) of water. Simmer for 10 minutes, blend and return to the saucepan.

2 To make the tagine, heat 2 tablespoons of oil in a large pan. Brown the meat and the onions. Stir in the ginger, chilli, paprika, cinnamon, flour and garlic. Give it about 30 seconds before adding the tomatoes, stock cube, sultanas and 425ml (¾ pint) of water.

3 About half an hour before your guests are due, preheat the oven to 170°C/325°F/gas mark 3. When it's hot put the tagine in. It takes about 1½ hours to cook.

4 Crush the amaretti biscuits to crumbs and sprinkle half of over the base of the pastry case. (NB: these cases are very fragile.) Beat the eggs and stir in the cream, castor sugar and 3 tablespoons of calvados, or whichever spirit you're using. Mix in the almonds and the rest of the amaretti crumbs. Cut the apples in half horizontally and take the cores out. Put them, cut side up, in an ovenproof dish. Stuff the centre with sultanas, put a knob of butter on top of each one and sprinkle with brown sugar and the remaining calvados. Leave the pastry case, cream filling and apples to one side.

5 To serve the starter, gently reheat the soup and pop the poppadums in the hot oven for a couple of minutes to warm through. Fill a couple of small bowls with mango chutney (one for each end of the table). When you've dished up the soup get someone else to carry it (and the poppudums) to your guests and stir the beans into the tagine. And of course, don't even think of leaving the kitchen without boiling a kettle – you'll need it for the couscous, although it could be a useful prop for:

sperm whale (p72)

THE MEAL CONT...

meanwhile, back to the kitchen...

Give yourself 5 minutes to cook the couscous and get the pudding under way.

6 While one of your guests displays just how graphic their imagination really is, cook the couscous according to the instructions on the packet. Pour the cream mixture into the pastry case (don't overfill as it will rise slightly) and put in the oven along with the apples. The pud takes 20 minutes to cook, so don't forget about it. Stir the butter, cucumber, coriander and spring onions into the couscous. Dish up. Serve the tagine on top of the couscous and sprinkle over the pistachios. You could do this in the kitchen or at the table, but remember that the tagine will be very hot.

meanwhile, back to the kitchen...

Don't start playing the Association game until you've taken the tart and baked apples out of the oven – you don't want to serve them baking hot. Check the tart is pretty solid in the middle before you switch the oven off.

Kitchen business over, relax and enjoy some...

association (p72)

7 Cut the tart into thin slices with a very sharp knife. Serve everyone a piece of the tart with an apple half arranged artistically beside it. Pour some of the buttery juices from the dish over each apple. When you've finished eating, it's time to pucker up again.

lips united (p73)

Lavinia played the coquette with the popadums…

SPERM WHALE

you will need

At least one gullible guest
An accomplice

aim of the game

To force one guest to reveal to the assembled company some deep-seated sexual perceptions!

how to play

Explain to your guests that you're going to be playing a game of 'animal charades'. Ask someone (your intended victim) to go first, and take them out of the room. Tell them that they have to act out 'Sperm Whale'. Meanwhile, while you are out of the room, your accomplice tells all the other guests that X is going to come back and act a sperm whale and what ever they do they are not to guess it.

The poor victim then prances around the room desperately using all their dramatic abilities to act out sperm whale to a group of people determined not to utter the words sperm whale!

tips

Keep a bottle of washing up liquid handy – after 5 minutes you can let the victim use props!

ASSOCIATION

you will need

Like-minded minds

aim of the game

To build a chain of associated words around the table.

how to play

Choose a noun, any noun, to start with, although subsequent words can be any part of speech. The person to your left must immediately say a word that has an obvious association. e.g. You start with 'House', your neighbour says 'Roof', their neighbour says 'Fiddler' etc. Any faltering, repetition or non-association means a forfeit.

tips

The saying 'A good game is a quick game' holds true here – the faster, the better.
If you happen to have a bunch of rocket scientists round for dinner then you can make the game a little harder by categorizing the association – so you could have names of footballers, cars, flora and fauna etc.

LIPS UNITED

what you need

8 pairs of luscious lips – attached to uninhibited owners
A very good blindfold
Handcuffs *(or a tea towel)*

aim of the game

To identify whose lips are whose.

how to play

Everyone stands in a circle. The first person 'on' is then blindfolded and has their hands handcuffed or tied with the tea towel behind their back (so they can't discover the identity of the person they're kissing by touching them). Spin the blindfolded person in the centre of the circle 10 times. They then stagger to the perimeter of the assembled group, pucker up and give the first person they bump into a good kiss. The kisser has one attempt at guessing whose body the lips belong to: if they are correct they return to the middle of the ring for another 10 spins and another chance for a good smacker. If they can't guess whose lips they've kissed then person number 2 has a go and so on.

tips

Give yourself a high number so that you have more time to research everyone's kissing technique.
Inviting a large number of ex-lovers gives an unfair advantage – although it may make for an uncomfortable evening in other ways. (And think carefully before revealing to the assembled company that you own a pair of handcuffs…)

A 10-MINUTE DINNER

in which our friends ask a lot of questions

This is the dinner party for the times when you've got a nasty feeling you may still be stuck in a meeting 5 minutes before your guests are due. It will taste like you've made a huge effort – but really does take only minutes. NB! Don't throw all your newspapers out – you'll need them…

THE MENU

SODA BREAD 'PIZZAS'

who the devil am i?

BAKED HALIBUT WITH RICE NOODLES AND KOMBU BROTH

are you there, moriarty?

STICKY BUTTERED BANANAS WITH ICE CREAM

the ice cube game

"The game took longer than expected because Topsy had never heard of Mickey Mouse..."

THE SHOPPING

S the pizzas

8 soda bread farls *(or plain muffins)*
3 tablespoons pesto
3 tablespoons sun-dried tomato paste
4 round soft goat's cheeses
8 cherry tomatoes

M baked halibut

4 carrots
2 leeks
100g (3½oz) oyster mushrooms
4 strips of kombu *(Japanese seaweed or a handful of spinach)*
500ml (18fl oz) fish stock
2 teaspoons ginger paste
500g (1lb 2oz) rice noodles
8 halibut steaks *(use cod if you're on a budget)*
soy sauce

P sticky bananas

100g (3½oz) butter
8 tablespoons demerara sugar
400ml (14 fl oz)orange juice
4 tablespoons sultanas
4 tablespoons dark rum
8 bananas
500g (1lb 2oz) good ice cream

TO PREPARE THE MEAL

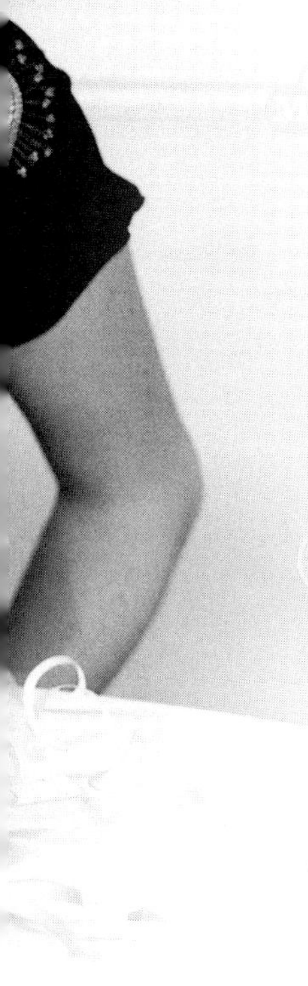

1 Turn the grill on to a medium heat. Fill and boil a kettle (of course). Cut the farls in half horizontally and spread 8 of the cut surfaces with the pesto and 8 with sun-dried tomato paste. Slice each of the goat's cheeses into 4 discs and place a disc on each piece of farl. Halve the cherry tomatoes and put a half on the tip of each farl.

2 Peel the carrots and cut into long batons. Cut the pale part of each leek into long strips and tear the mushrooms into strips too. Snip the kombu into chunks. Put the fish stock, 1 litre (1¾ pints) of water, the ginger, carrots, leeks, mushrooms and kombu in a large lidded pan. Cover and put the pan on a very low heat.

3 Pop the farls under the grill and serve as soon as the surface of the cheese starts to change colour and texture. Don't let the bread burn – and get your brain ticking over....

who the devil am i? (p80)

meanwhile, back to the kitchen

Once you've had your go, leave the others to get on with the game while you cook; obviously they'll only get 6 questions each, but tough.

4 Reboil the kettle and put the rice noodles in a large, heatproof container. Pour the water over and leave them to soak for 4 minutes (or as according to the instructions on the packet).

5 Turn the heat up slightly under the pan with the vegetables in and slide in the fish steaks. Keep the pan covered. (If your pan's not big enough to hold all 8, do 4 at a time, keeping the cooked ones warm under the grill.) The fish will only take about 3 minutes to cook through.

6 Drain the noodles and place on plates or in bowls. Put a piece of fish on top with some of the veg and broth from the pan. Serve with soy sauce on the table. After enjoying, it's time to play:

THE MEAL CONT...

are you there, Moriarty? (p80)

meanwhile, back to the kitchen...

Moriarty players can happily be left whacking each other while you return to the cooker for 5 minutes to make the pud.

Gently melt the butter in a large frying pan. Stir in sugar, juice, sultanas and rum. Turn up the heat and let it bubble while you slice the bananas. Mix in bananas and cook for a couple of minutes. Serve with a dollop of ice cream. And while you're at the freezer grab a tray of ice cubes for the imaginatively titled...

ice cube game (p81)

The noodles were so delicious that Bunty totally forgot her manners

WHO THE DEVIL AM I? ☺

you will need

8 small pieces of paper or Post-It notes
8 pens
Good bit of spit

aim of the game

To guess the name stuck on your forehead by only asking questions that can be answered yes or no.

how to play

Everyone writes down the name of a well-known, or famous, person – it could even be someone around the table or just some old dear from the pub who's known to you all. Then stick it on the forehead of the person on your left.
When it's your go ask each person one question about who you are – i.e. you have just 7 questions to get it right. If you haven't worked it out by then, quite frankly, you're hopeless.

tips

Remember to ask the obvious questions like 'Am I alive?', 'Am I a woman?' etc.
Don't let anyone deviate from 'yes' or 'no' answers.

ARE YOU THERE, MORIARTY? ⊗

you will need

2 Blindfolds
2 copies of the Sunday Times
(any paper will do but a broadsheet has more clout)
A good sense of hearing
(and we suppose a sense of humour is beneficial as well)

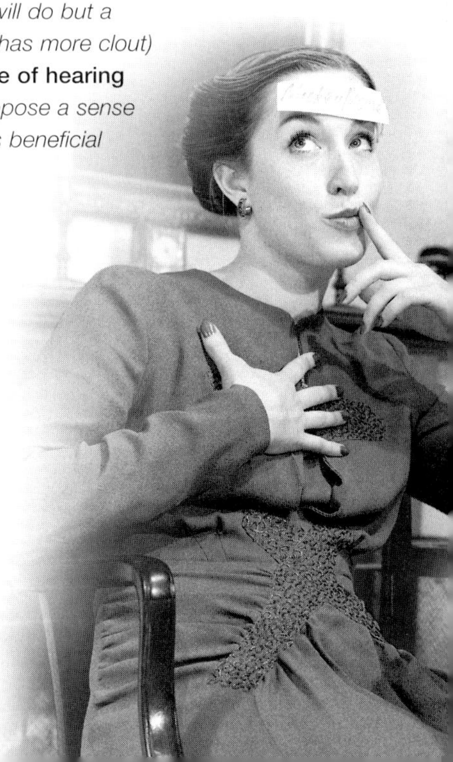

THE ICE CUBE GAME

aim of the game

To hit your opponent over the head with a rolled-up newspaper while blindfolded and lying on the floor.

how to play

Truss up 2 of your guests with the blindfolds – it's imperative that they can't see a thing. They lie on the floor, face down and head to head, holding each other's left hand. In their other hand they hold the rolled-up section of the bumper-edition newspaper.

The first person calls, 'Are you there, Moriarty?' to which the other player must answer 'Yes'. The first person swipes at where he thinks his opponent is lying, attempting to whack them on the head. A successful strike earns another go. An unsuccessful strike means the opponent gets a chance to have a crack. The game ends when someone concedes defeat or the papers have been shredded.

tip

When replying to the call either throw your voice or roll over subtly.

you will need

A few ice cubes (if you want to have more than one round)
Fanciable guests either side of you

aim of the game

Obviously to get a snog – cunningly disguised as passing the ice cube from person to person using your mouth!

how to play

Place the ice cube between your teeth and pass it to the person on your left. They then turn to their left and pass it on. It gets more risque as the ice cube melts.

tips

Don't allow anyone to swallow the ice cube – you don't want to run out of props. Encourage your guests to hold the ice cube between their teeth, not in their mouths – hygiene is an issue here. (You may be wise to stock up on toothpaste for sensitive teeth to

CORNERSHOP AND CUPBOARD

in which we have unexpected visitors!

This is perfect for that panicky moment when you realize that the people you invited over for a drink after work aren't going home, you're going to have to feed them and the cupboard is virtually bare. However sparse the stock in your late night corner shop, you should be able to rustle up this lot.

THE MENU

cereal thriller

BAKED TORTILLAS

pass the matchbox

BALSAMIC ONION AND SPICY SAUSAGE PASTA

the chocolate game

Marjorie completely disgraced herself in the chocolate game...

THE SHOPPING

S baked tortillas

2 large bags of tortilla chips
jar of salsa
tub of guacamole *(optional)*
bag of ready grated cheese or lump of cheddar

M the pasta

500g pasta shells or other shapes
12 meaty, thick-skinned sausages
8 rashers bacon, cut into strips
400g tin of tomatoes
4 medium sized onions
1-2 teaspoon chilli powder
2 tablespoons balsamic vinegar
2 tablespoons olive oil & extra if necessary

P pudding

the biggest bar of milk chocolate in the shop.

TO PREPARE THE MEAL

While you're shopping your guests get a workout with:

cereal thriller (p86)

1 Preheat the grill to medium heat. Peel the onions and slice into fine rings. Fry gently in the oil for 10 minutes. While this happens skin the sausages and finely chop the meat inside. Add the vinegar to the onions and turn up the heat. Allow most of the liquid to boil off before adding the bacon and sausage meat. Boil the kettle for the pasta.

2 Arrange half the tortillas on a large, heatproof plate. Dollop with guacamole or half the salsa. Put the rest of the tortillas on top, dollop on salsa and top with grated cheese. Grill until the cheese melts.

3 Dump the tin of tomatoes on top of the meat (which should be browning by now). Reduce the heat and leave to cook. Let everyone help themselves to tortillas and grab a matchbox for:

pass the match box (p86)

meanwhile, back to the kitchen...

The pasta will take about 10 minutes (check the instructions on the packet) so head back to the cooker when your guests have got the hang of the game.

4 Cook the pasta as per instructions and give the tomato mixture a good stir. It should start to get fairly thick (you're aiming to coat the pasta, not have gallons of sauce). In the meantime make the salad by chopping the cucumber and tomatoes into very small chunks. Peel the carrots and do the same to them. Mix in the olives, pulses (drained and rinsed) and nuts. Whisk together the vinegar and mustard and slowly add the oil to make the dressing. Drizzle over the salad.

5 Once the pasta is cooked, drain it and chuck it back into the saucepan. Pour over the sausage mixture and give it all a really good stir. Serve up on to warm plates or bowls.

6 The pudding is...

the chocolate game! (p87)

CEREAL THRILLER

you will need

Elasticated legs
Cereal packet *(remove the contents first)*

aim of the game

To pick up the cereal packet using only your mouth: sounds easy enough, until you realize that every time you've all had a go, an inch is ripped off the top of the packet and only the soles of your feet can touch the floor. So stretch those thigh muscles and show off how supple you are.

how to play

Place the cereal packet in the middle of the floor. Each person then has, in turn, to pick up the packet using their mouth without letting their hands, or legs, touch the ground. After everyone in the room has successfully picked it up, tear off about an inch of cardboard from the top of the packet. Now repeat the process; if someone admits defeat then they're out. Eventually you will have a flat piece of cardboard on the ground – the winner is the one remaining person who hasn't admitted defeat.

tips

Use of tongue is permitted (it'll give you an extra inch!).
Play it on a non-slippery surface.
Discourage players from slobbering on the cardboard.
Your thighs will be agony the following day.

PASS THE MATCHBOX

you will need

8 good sized conks
1 small matchbox *(unless you've got Gerard Depardieu and Barry Manilow round your table in which case "cook's matches" might be advisable!)*

aim of the game

To pass the outer covering of a matchbox from person to person using only noses!

THE GAMES CONT...

how to play

Remove the inside of the matchbox and put aside (you never know when you might want toothpicks). Place the outer casing on the end of your nose and pass it to the person next to you. They insert their nose in the other end and take it from you. Failure to pass or receive it involves both parties having a drinking forfeit.

tip

It's not nice playing with people who have colds or hay fever.

THE CHOCOLATE GAME ☺

you will need

Hat
Scarf
Coat
Gloves
Knife and fork
A dice
A big bar of chocolate
A tray

aim of the game

To stuff yourself with chocolate!

how to play

Sit in a circle on the floor with the chocolate bar on a tray in the middle. Take it in turns to throw the dice. Every time someone throws a 6 they have to don the hat, scarf, coat and gloves, then tuck into the chocolate using the knife and fork. Meanwhile, everyone else tries to throw a 6. As soon as they do, the person munching away has to de-robe and hand over the gear.

tips

If your carpet is precious, it might be worth putting down some newspaper under the chocolate as it tends to fly everywhere.
The colder the chocolate, the harder it is to chop up.
Don't be disappointed if you don't get chocolate every go. On the other hand, if you get stuck with the chocolate while everyone else fails to throw a 6, you've got to keep eating no matter how sick you feel – admitting defeat just isn't playing the game!

A BRILLIANT BARBECUE

in which our friends get a bit tied up

Once in a while the sun does shine enough to tempt us out into the garden. Let other people do burgers – this is much more sophisticated, but not a lot more complicated. Remember it will take at least half an hour to get the barbie to the point where you can cook: it must have stopped flaming, but the coals should be glowing red hot.

THE MENU

BAKED BRIE WITH ROSEMARY

bondage

CHICKEN SKEWERS, VEGETABLE KEBABS & MARINATED PORK FILLETS WITH BEAN AND GRILLED RED PEPPER SALAD, & HOT HOME-MADE TOMATO SALSA

round the baseball bat

HONEY-GRILLED PINEAPPLE

the game

Johnny and Susan had no problems coping with bondage, but Freddie and Topsy got in a terrible muddle…

THE SHOPPING

S baked brie

1 large wedge of brie
few sprigs of rosemary
silver foil
lots of tortilla chips

M the barbeque

2 tablespoons brown sugar
150g (5oz) rice vinegar
2 teaspoons Chinese five-spice powder
4 cloves of garlic, peeled and crushed
4 tablespoons soy sauce
8 pork steaks
150ml (¼ pint) olive oil
juice of 2 limes
3 teaspoons paprika
2 teaspoons cumin
2 teaspoons ground coriander
6 skinless chicken breasts
3 green peppers
3 courgettes
250g (9oz) closed-cup mushrooms
500g (1lb 2oz) black beans
3 red peppers
2 tablespoons balsamic vinegar
6 tablespoons olive oil
wooden skewers
8 well-flavoured tomatoes
1 red onion, peeled
1 red chilli, de-seeded
bunch of coriander, chopped
2 or 3 baguettes

P the pineapple

2 ready-prepared pineapples
4 tablespoons runny honey

TO PREPARE THE MEAL

1. The secret of a good barbecue is well-marinated food, so start early – preferably the day before. The black beans need to be soaked overnight, but If you can't start early, use tinned pulses instead.

2. Start with the pork. In a small saucepan dissolve the brown sugar in the rice vinegar. Add the Chinese five-spice powder, 2 crushed garlic cloves and 2 tablespoons of the soy sauce. Bring to the boil and pour over the pork steaks in a shallow dish. Leave to cool until required. Turn the steaks occasionally.

3. Make the kebab marinade next. Stir together 150ml olive oil, the lime juice, remaining garlic, paprika, cumin and coriander. Cube the chicken and green peppers. Slice the courgettes into chunks and wipe the mushrooms. Put the chicken and veg into the marinade and leave for several hours. (If you're entertaining vegetarians marinate the meat and veg in separate dishes.) Cook the beans according to the instructions (you must boil them for at least 10 minutes; they need about 35 minutes cooking time in total).

4. Top, tail and de-seed the red peppers so you're left with a flat slice of pepper flesh. If the barbie's going at this point put them skin side down so that the skin blackens and blisters. If it's not, do the same thing under a hot grill (but with the skin side up, obviously). When they're done, chuck them in a plastic bag for 15 minutes: sounds strange, but it steams the skin off. Peel and slice, then mix into the rinsed and drained beans. Dress with remaining soy sauce, balsamic vinegar and 4 tablespoons of olive oil.

5. An hour or so before you're ready to go chuck the wooden skewers into a bowl of water – they need to soak for about 30 minutes to stop them burning. For the salsa, finely chop the tomatoes, red onion and chilli and mix with a good handful of coriander. Splash on a couple of tablespoons of olive oil and chill until needed.

6. Make up the kebabs by fishing the veg and chicken

THE MEAL CONT...

out of their marinade and threading on to the soaked, wooden skewers. Keep the meat and vegetables separate as the chicken takes slightly longer to cook.

7 Cut the top off the brie, put a sprig of rosemary on top of the skinned cheese and replace the top. Wrap in silver foil, tucking sprigs of rosemary around it as you go. Put on the barbecue, skinned side down, for about 5 minutes. Peel back the top and serve with tortilla chips to scoop out the lovely gooey cheese. Let everyone tuck in while you get tied up with...

bondage (p94)

meanwhile, back to the barbie...

Leave everyone tied up and put the chicken and the pork steaks on the barbie. Depending on the heat they'll take 5-7 minutes each side. It's crucial that they are cooked through properly. Put the pork marinade in a small saucepan and reheat on the side of the grill.

8 Cook the veg kebabs in the same way as the chicken, but only give them a couple of minutes each side. Serve with the salads and French bread. Untie anyone who hasn't worked out Bondage yet – they shouldn't have to starve.

Time to burn off all that food, with...

round the baseball bat (p94)

meanwhile, back to the barbie...

Pudding's simple – lucky really as you won't be capable of much once you've been round the baseball bat a few times.

9 Cut the pineapples into thick rings, discarding the central core. Brush with honey and grill on the dying embers of the barbie for a couple of minutes each side or until they just start to brown round the edges.

the game (p95)

"*Everyone agreed that it was a cracking barbecue...*"

BONDAGE ☺

you will need

String

aim of the game

To untangle yourself from your partner without untying the string.

how to play

Cut 2 lengths of string (each about 1 metre or 1 yard long) and tie one piece around both wrists of one of your guests (so they're effectively handcuffed with it). Take the other length, loop it over the first piece and tie the ends to the wrists of another guest. Tell them that they have to untangle themselves without untying the string. Sit back and laugh!

tips

The trick is: it's got nothing to do with stepping under or over each other, backward somersaults in unison or showing off your suppleness.
Simply make a small loop from your bondage partner's string and without twisting it thread it through the 'cuff' on your left hand, going from your wrist towards your fingers. Slide your hand through the loop and bingo you're free!

ROUND THE BASEBALL BAT ⊗

you will need

2 baseball bats *(hockey sticks or tennis racquets will suffice)*

aim of the game

To win – it's a relay race.

how to play

Divide into 2 teams. Mark a start position and place the 2 bats about 30 metres (30 yards) away. On 'Start' the first team member has to run from the start position to the baseball bat. They stand the bat up, bend over it placing their head on the other end and run around it 20 times. They then try to run back in a straight line and touch the next team member so they can repeat the process.

THE GAMES CONT...

tips

Don't play in an enclosed area.
Play on grass.
Don't be surprised if you feel dizzy.
Keep a close eye on both teams to make sure that everyone is circling the baseball bat 20 times.

THE GAME ☺

you will need

2 teams
A clock with a second hand
An area for one of the teams to deliberate in

aim of the game

To act out to your team the subject given to you by the other team. It's like a cross between the *Hat Game*, *Give Us A Clue* and *Charades*.

how to play

Divide your guests into 2. Separate the 2 teams while they think of titles from books, plays, TV programmes or films – one for each member of the opposite team. The first person from Team B is given their title by Team A. They have two minutes to act it out to their team (i.e. Team B). Team B then give the first member of Team A their title etc.

tip

Remember that you don't want to give the opposition easy titles as you want to win, but it does get boring if you pick obscure titles that no one knows.
Make sure that you whisper the title to the person on the other team who will be acting!

A PERFECT PICNIC

in which a wine bottle finds another use

Everyone loves a picnic. This one is smart enough for a big event and simple enough for a gang of friends on a day out. Bear in mind that people use being outdoors as an excuse to eat loads more than usual, so don't be afraid to pad this out with shop-bought goodies like dips, fresh cooked prawns, mini scotch eggs etc. Don't forget some secure containers, a sharp knife, a corkscrew and a rug or two.

THE MENU

ROAST VEGETABLE ROLLS

volleyball

TARRAGON CHICKEN WITH RISOTTO CAKE AND ORANGE SALAD

kick the can

CHOCOLATE MINI BAR LOAF AND FRUIT

pass the bottle

"It was with utter glee that they opened Freddie's basket..."

THE SHOPPING

S vegetable rolls

6 courgettes
2 large aubergines
4 red peppers
olive oil
8 large crusty rolls
4 tablespoons tomato pesto
4 balls (400g or 14oz) of mozzarella, sliced

M tarragon chicken

250g (9oz) risotto rice
4 eggs
4 tablespoons grated pecorino
300g (11oz) jar of mushrooms in oil, drained *(but keep the oil)*
8 chicken breasts
bunch of fresh tarragon
2 bay leaves
6 tablespoons balsamic vinegar
juice and rind of 2½ oranges
olive oil
juice of ½ lemon
large bag of salad leaves

P mini bar loaf

200g (7oz) milk chocolate
2 tubes of Smarties
25 mini chocolate bars *(Mars, Crunchie, Bounty, Twirl etc.)*
150g (5oz) bag of Maltesers
fresh fruit *(e.g. cherries or strawberries)*

TO PREPARE THE MEAL

1 Start with pud. Slowly melt the milk chocolate in a saucepan. Put a layer of Smarties in the bottom of a small loaf tin. Arrange a layer of mini chocolate bars on top (it doesn't matter which flavour goes next to which – the idea is to get a different taste every time you chop a bit off). Then add a layer of Maltesers. Then more chocolate bars, until the loaf tin is full. Pour the melted chocolate into the tin, trying to fill the gaps between the mini bars. Stand the tin in hot water (just plonk it in the sink) for about 5 minutes: you want the chocolate to soften enough so the bars stick together, without melting so much that it all turns into a gunky mess. Refrigerate until needed and enjoy the leftover choccy bars.

2 Put the oven on to heat to 200°C/400°F/gas mark 6. Make the risotto up according to the packet instructions, but don't overcook it – the rice should still have bite to it. Beat the eggs, season well and stir in with the pecorino and drained mushrooms (keep the oil for the salad dressing). Oil a 20-23cm (8-9in) cake tin and slop in the rice mixture. It'll look disgusting at this stage, but don't worry. Bake for 30 minutes. Let it cool and transport it in its tin.

3 While the onven's on, get the starter going. Cut the courgettes and aubergines into long thin slices. De-seed and slice the peppers. Don't worry if it looks like you've got tons of veg – it cooks down very quickly. Put them in a large roasting tin with a liberal dousing of olive oil and bake for about 20 minutes (or until they're very soft). Stir occasionally.

4 You may as well chuck the chicken breasts in the oven too. Put them in a deep roasting dish, cover with boiling water, throw in a few sprigs of tarragon and a couple of bay leaves. They should be done at the same time as the veg. Discard the poaching liquid and allow the chicken to cool before cutting into chunks.

5 Make a dressing for the chicken by boiling the balsamic vinegar with the juice and grated rind of 2 oranges until it's reduced by half. Take off the heat and mix in an equal quantity of olive

THE MEAL CONT...

oil. When it's cool stir in 2 tablespoons of chopped tarragon and pour over the chicken.

M 6 Make a dressing for the salad by mixing the juice of half an orange, half a lemon and 3 tablespoons of the oil from the mushrooms. Season well and put into a small plastic container. Take the salad in its supermarket bag.

S 7 When the roast veggies are cool, slice the tops off the rolls and hollow out inside, leaving a good coating of bread. Spread the inside roughly with pesto, then fill with layers of vegetables and mozzarella slices. Replace the tops and wrap each roll tightly in foil.

S P M 8 When you're packing up your cool box ready to go, put the rolls on the bottom (they need to squish down so the flavours blend). Keep the pudding and chicken coldest. Freeze cartons of fruit juice before you go. They'll keep everything extra cold and provide lovely slushy drinks when you start the picnic.

S P M 9 When you arrive, serve some drinks while they're still cold, pitch your volleyball net and dish up the food whenever you've worked up an appetite. Unwrap the rolls, cut the risotto cake into slices and keep the mini-bar loaf cool until you need a chocolate hit after Kick the Can. Serve it with fresh fruit and let guests chop chunks off it themselves.

NB! Don't throw out the inside of the bread rolls – chuck the spare crumbs in the freezer and use them when you want to make chocolate apple charlotte (p114)

When Minnie accepted the invitation to the picnic she had not realised what was at stake...

McCUNE-STYLE VOLLEYBALL

you will need

Volleyball net *(they're quite cheap, but string between two posts will do)*
Volleyball ball, or a lightweight football
Two teams

aim of the game

To win (first to 15 points).

how to play

Put the net up and mark out the pitch. (The boundaries should be about ten paces from the posts.)
To score a point the team has to be serving.
To serve: hold the ball in the palm of one hand and give it a good whack with the other so as it goes over the net. If it hits the net on the way over it's a 'let'. If the serve doesn't make it over the net, or goes out, or even hits a fellow team member, then the serve goes to the opposition.
The ball is hit using one or both of your hands.
When a team wins the right to serve each team member rotates one to the left.
The ball is volleyed between the 2 teams: unlike tennis the ball can be hit up to 3 times by 1 team before going over the net, as long as the same player doesn't hit it twice consecutively.

CROOK-STYLE TOWEL VOLLEYBALL

you will need

As above, plus several large towels (one for every 2 players)

how to play

Play as above but put players in pairs within the team. Each pair holds a towel taut between them, using this as their means to hit the ball over the net.

KICK THE CAN

you will need

A good expanse of varied terrain
A can – any size

aim of the game

For the person who's 'It' to 'capture' all other players.

how to do it

Choose a person to be 'It'. They count to 100 while everyone else dashes off and hides. The person who's 'It' scouts around. Hiders are 'caught' when 'It' has spotted them, run back to the can, kicked it and said: 'I see X behind the rose bushes.' Captives must stand by the can and are only freed if another player gets to the can and kicks it before 'It' does.
Once everyone is caught the first captive becomes the next 'It'.

tips

Limit the boundaries.
Watch out for nettles when hiding.
Make sure that 'It' doesn't lurk by the can all the time – they must go out and look for the other player.

PASS THE BOTTLE

you will need

2 teams
2 empty bottles

aim of the game

To pass the bottle between each team member, only using your legs. First team to finish wins.

how to play

The 2 teams line up, each with a bottle on the ground in front of the first member. They have to pick up the bottle using their knees, turn and pass to the next team member. If the bottle's dropped anywhere along the line the whole team has to start again.

tips

Skirts and tights are a disadvantage!

A WILD WEEKEND AWAY

in which the countryside beckons

This seems to have a huge shopping list, but it does cover all your meals and some items like double cream and chilli flakes are listed twice. We'd chuck in about 20 pieces of fruit, a few jumbo packs of biscuits and crisps for munchies, plus soft drinks. Before you set off for the supermarket, check whether you need to take loo roll, bin liners and washing up liquid with you on your weekend away.

The best way to organize the bills is for one person to do all the food shopping and then split the bill between everybody else. You could do the same thing with the booze, or you could get all your guests to bring all the alcohol they think they'll need for a weekend. (Remind them this will probably be a lot.)

You'll need a good cool box to transport the food. Wedge the ice packs around the ice cream and any other frozen food you're taking.

Make sure everyone has a map and details of the exact address of the location and any useful mobile numbers so you can stay in touch on the way. Ask guests to bring fancy dress for Saturday night's entertainment, the Ambassador's Reception. Kitsch seventies cocktailwear looks good, but we also had a terrorist one year! Encourage guests to car-share. When you send out the details of the weekend make sure everyone also gets a copy of what they'll need to find on the Scavenger Hunt.

"Lavinia thought that this trophy might just give her the scavenger hunt prize..."

THE WEEKEND'S MENUS

FRIDAY NIGHT

scavenger hunt

SAUSAGES AND PUY LENTILS WITH SALAD
AND GRILLED POLENTA

l'orange dangereuse

CHEESE BOARD

SATURDAY BREAKFAST

FRY UP

SATURDAY LUNCH

CHARCUTERIE, CHEESE AND SALADS

french cricket

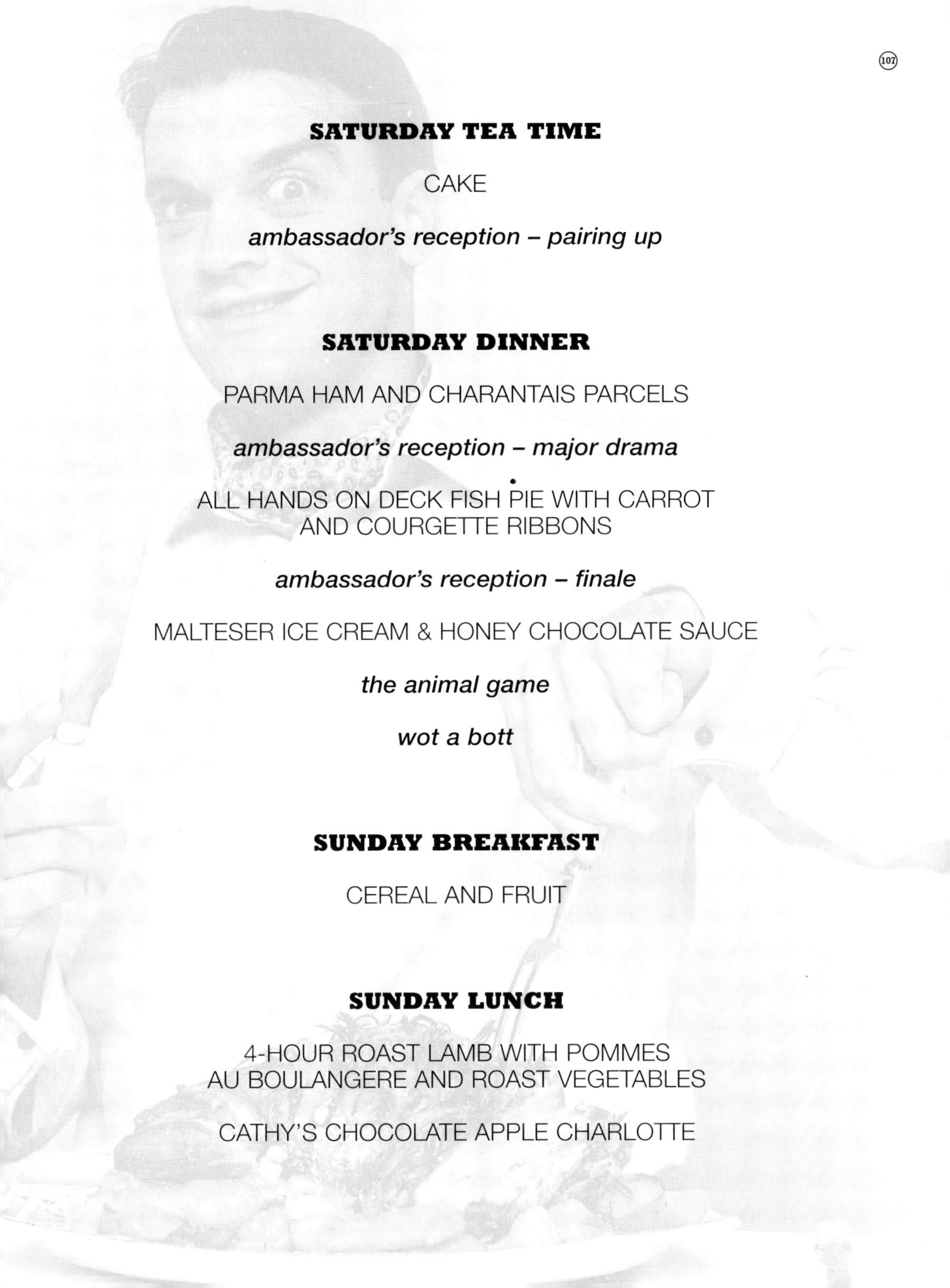

SATURDAY TEA TIME

CAKE

ambassador's reception – pairing up

SATURDAY DINNER

PARMA HAM AND CHARANTAIS PARCELS

ambassador's reception – major drama

ALL HANDS ON DECK FISH PIE WITH CARROT AND COURGETTE RIBBONS

ambassador's reception – finale

MALTESER ICE CREAM & HONEY CHOCOLATE SAUCE

the animal game

wot a bott

SUNDAY BREAKFAST

CEREAL AND FRUIT

SUNDAY LUNCH

4-HOUR ROAST LAMB WITH POMMES AU BOULANGERE AND ROAST VEGETABLES

CATHY'S CHOCOLATE APPLE CHARLOTTE

THE SHOPPING

Friday Dinner

cooking oil
4 onions
24 big, good-quality sausages
2 yellow peppers
2 red peppers
1 red chilli
500g (1lb 2oz) Puy lentils
700g (1½lb) passata
2 glasses of red wine
4 teaspoons dried oregano
500g (1lb 2oz) polenta
400g (14oz) salad leaves
8 tomatoes
a small bottle of olive oil
2 tablespoons balsamic vinegar
2 oranges

2 different types of crackers for cheese
around 200g (7oz) each of 4 different cheeses *(try to choose one hard cheese, like a well-flavoured cheddar; a goat's cheese; a blue cheese and one other that you fancy)*
butter
a few Cox apples

Saturday Breakfast

20 rashers of lean bacon
16 eggs
4 x 400g (14oz) tins of baked beans
600g (1¼lb) mushrooms
3 large sliced loaves
butter or margarine
350g jar of marmalade
350g jar of jam
100g jar of instant coffee
50 tea bags
4.5 litres (8 pints) milk

Saturday Lunch

3 baguettes
last night's cheese
200g (7oz) pâté
400g cold meats
400g coleslaw
2 bags of green salad
400g (14oz) jar of mayonnaise
400g (14oz) tinned tuna in brine
400g (14oz) tinned sweetcorn

Saturday Tea

1 large squishy cake or a selection of kiddie tea-time treats like: Waggon Wheels, Jammy Dodgers, Fondant Fancies etc

THE SHOPPING CONTINUED...

Saturday Dinner

2 ripe Charentais melons
250g Parma ham

200g (7oz) (frozen) prawns
400g (14oz) fresh haddock *(get the fishmonger to skin it for you)*
400g (14oz) smoked haddock
800ml (28fl oz) milk
2 bay leaves
500g (1lb 2oz) potatoes
500g (1lb 2oz) sweet potato
400g (14oz) leeks
50g (2oz) butter – *plus extra for mashed potato*
50g (2oz) plain flour
250g (9oz) carrots
6 courgettes
1 teaspoon chilli flakes

1 litre (1¾ pint) vanilla ice-cream
150g (5oz) Maltesers
1 box Ferrero Rocher
200g (7oz) plain chocolate (at least 55% cocoa solids)
4 tablespoons runny honey
4 tablespoons double cream

Sunday Breakfast

large packet of cereal
painkillers

Sunday Lunch

cooking oil
3kg (7lb) leg of lamb
small bunch of rosemary
4 cloves of garlic, peeled and sliced
400g (14oz) onions
400g (14oz) carrots
4 bay leaves
1 bottle of dry white wine
silver foil
1kg (2¼lb) roasting potatoes
3 aubergines
6 red or yellow peppers
4 tablespoons olive oil
1 large Savoy cabbage
2 teaspoons coriander seeds, crushed
1 teaspoon dried chilli flakes
2 tablespoons balsamic vinegar
a few basil leaves

1½kg (3½lb) cooking apples
12 slices white bread
150g (5oz) butter
6 tablespoons caster sugar
6 tablespoons cocoa powder (not drinking chocolate)
50g (2oz) plain chocolate drops
550ml (1 pint) double cream

SCAVENGER HUNT ☺

you will need

A list of objects to be found

aim of the game

To break up the journey and break the ice when people arrive.

how to do it

Give each driver a list of 10 objects that they have to pick up on their journey such as:
a Little Chef napkin, coloured condoms, a gobstopper, a gladioli, a paper doily, disposable knickers, box of matches from a designated hotel/restaurant etc.

tips

You could also ask teams to gather information, like the name of the barmaid in the village pub.
Don't make it too complicated; everyone will want to get to their destination as quickly as possible.
Players have to explain where they found cach item – drinking forfeits for cheaty cheats who bought stuff before they hit the road.

FRIDAY'S MEAL

If you were incredibly organized, you could make the sausage dish beforehand, seal it very well and take it with you. If you're not that organized (and not that many of us are) send your guests off to compare scavenger hunt trophies at the pub and get cooking.

1. Rescue the ice-cream from your cool bag and empty into a bowl. Lightly crush the Maltesers and stir into the ice cream. Re-freeze for tomorrow.

2. Heat a couple of tablespoons of cooking oil in a large pan. Peel and chop the onions and cook gently for about 10 minutes. Then add the sausages and turn up the heat a bit so they start to brown. De-seed and slice the peppers and chilli, add them to the pan with the lentils. Boil a kettle of water.

3. Let it all cook for a couple of minutes, then stir in the passata, red wine, half the oregano and a wine glass of water. Cover and cook on a very low heat for 1 hour – stirring occassionally when you remember to.

4. Make the polenta, following the instructions on the packet. Stir the rest of the oregano into the mixture. Once it's cooked, spread on a lightly oiled baking sheet (or a couple of large plates). You're looking for a slab of polenta about 2-3cm (1in) thick.

5. Chuck the salad leaves in a bowl, chop the tomatoes and add. Join the others in the pub.

6. When you get back, heat the grill to high, cut the polenta into wedges or chunks and grill until slightly crusty on each side. Mix 4 tablespoons of olive oil with the balsamic vinegar and dress the salad. Serve with the sausages and polenta. Make sure you've got a couple of oranges to hand for:

l'orange dangereuse (p117)

7. Serve the cheese on a platter with the crackers, butter and the apples. Leave everyone to chat – there will be plenty more games this weekend.

SATURDAY'S MEALS

BREAKFAST

You've provided all the ingredients – let someone else do the cooking. Even the most culinarily challenged seem to be able to rustle up a fry up. Men who don't know one end of a tea-towel from the other pride themselves on doing a good breakfast. Give them the opportunity to show off their skills.

After breakfast rally the troops and get everyone out and about. It could be a good walk to build up a healthy appetite before lunch – or a longer adventure. Get people to take a packed lunch if you're going to be away from base into the afternoon. Take a ball and cozzies if you're going anywhere near water.

LUNCH

This is a compilation rather than an exercise in cooking. You may be going out for the day and want to take a picnic, or you may just be lazing around and can't be bothered to cook. Let people help themselves to:
baguettes; last night's cheese; pâté; charcuterie; coleslaw; green salad and mayonnaise. Drain and mix the tuna, sweetcorn and some mayo. Leave the fruit, biscuits and crisps lying around – and that's lunch. You don't want to waste time when you could be playing:

french cricket (p117)

TEA

If you're really keen, make a cake and take it with you. Otherwise just serve up a shop-bought one or a pile of fun kiddie biscuits and little cakes.

DINNER

M 1 Defrost the prawns for the fish pie if necessary.

M 2 The main course is called *All Hands On Deck Fish Pie* for a reason, so gather yourself at least four little helpers. Allocate one person responsibility for the fish, one for sweet potatoes, one for ordinary potatoes and one for leeks and white sauce. You can supervise.

THE MEALS CONT...

3 Fish Person needs to poach both types of fish together in the milk with the bay leaves. It will only take about 5 minutes (depending on the thickness of the fish) – it just needs to be flake-able, not overcooked. Get them to flake it into a large dish and chuck the prawns on top. Keep the milk (very important).

4 Both Potato Heads need to be busy peeling, chopping, boiling and mashing. It's important to keep the two types of potato separate so that you can create an artistically chequered topping of white and orange at the end. Get them to mash their potatoes with plenty of seasoning and butter (not milk, too runny).

5 Head of Leeks needs to clean, slice and sauté them in 50g (2oz) butter. Then sprinkle on the plain flour to make a roux (do it slowly as you don't want the leek sauce to be too thick). Gradually mix in the milk used for poaching to make a smooth sauce (you may not need all the milk). Pour on top of the fish mixture.

6 Now you can get creative and dollop on alternative spoonfuls of sweet and plain potato mash to make the topping. While you're being artistic, get one of your little helpers to cut the carrots and courgettes into long thin strips and chuck in a pan. (Good idea to get someone else to wash up, too!)

7 Starter will take seconds, main course just needs a reheat in the oven and pud's in the freezer. Time to explain the evening's entertainment...

the ambassador's reception (p118)

THE MEALS CONT...

8 While the couples ponder, assemble the starter. Cut the melons in half and de-seed. Cut each half into 4 and run a sharp knife between the flesh and the rind, so you end up with 16 de-rinded slices. Divide the Parma ham into 8 and wrap strips of it round the melon, 2 slices at a time. Serve. While you're eating the starter heat the oven for the fish pie to 220°C/425°F/gas mark 7.

9 Before the couples act out their scenarios go back to the kitchen and whack the fish pie in the oven: it will take 25 minutes. Boil a kettle.

Time for the performance. Vote on the most original ideas and choose 2 couples to go through to the finals. Give them another scenario to think about and get them to act it after the main course. The scenario is:
The caterers at the Ambassador's Reception have had a disaster and all they have to serve to the guests is chocolate.

10 Plunge the carrots and courgettes into boiling water for 2 minutes. Drain, sprinkle with salt, pepper and the chilli flakes. Serve with the fish pie.

The finalists act out their scenarios (still in character) and the winning team receives – surprise, surprise – a box of Ferrero Rocher.

11 While those chocs are being handed round make a chocolate sauce for the ice cream by melting the chocolate over a low heat and stirring in the runny honey and double cream. Pour a little over each portion of ice cream and serve immediately.

Forget the sophistication of the *Ambassador's Reception* now and get silly with one of the great games of all time:

the animal game (p118)

If it's late at night, the party's still swinging and the booze is still flowing this one could spice up your life:

wot a bott (p119)

SUNDAY'S MEALS

BREAKFAST

Let everyone help themselves to cereal, toast and fruit. You need to get started on the lamb.

LUNCH

M 1 It's called 4-hour lamb for a reason, so allow plenty of time (although it's pretty flexible and will be happy with anything between 3½ and five). Heat the oven to 170°C/325°F/gas mark 3. Heat 4 tablespoons of cooking oil in a large roasting pan. Fry the lamb until it's browned and then switch off the heat.

M 2 With a slim, sharp knife cut slits in the skin on top of the lamb and shove tiny rosemary sprigs and slices of garlic into the holes. Season all over. Peel and roughly chop the onions and carrots and arrange in the roasting tin around the lamb. Tuck in a couple of the bay leaves and pour over a bottle of white wine (hopefully you didn't drink it all on Saturday night). Add about 500ml (18fl oz) water (depending how deep your dish is) and bring to the boil. Take off the heat, cover with silver foil and put on the top shelf in the oven.

M 3 Before you head off for the brisk walk you need to cure your hangover get the veg and pudding ready too. Hopefully someone will have noticed that you're cooking again and offered to help. Get them to peel and thinly slice the spuds. To make pommes boulangere, butter a large heatproof dish and layer the potato slices with flakes of butter, salt and pepper. Pour over enough milk to cover about three quarters of the potatoes (volume depends on the depth of the dish you're using). Cover with foil.

M 4 Cut the aubergine and de-seeded peppers into large chunks, pour over 4 tablespoons of olive oil and mix around. Cover with foil. Shred the Savoy cabbage and plunge into boiling water for about 2 minutes. Refresh under a cold tap and leave to drain.

P 5 Set someone to work peeling, coring and slicing the cooking apples. Crumb the bread in a food

THE MEALS CONT...

processor, on a grater or with your hands. Fry the crumbs in the butter, stir in the sugar, cocoa powder and chocolate drops. Layer the apples and chocolate mixture, finishing with the choccie mix.

6 Just before heading outside put the potatoes on the middle shelf of the oven and the aubergine mixture on the bottom.

7 On your return, check everything is okay. Take the lamb out of the oven and allow it to rest (to make it easier to carve). Put the pudding in its place (it can cook at the same heat for anything between 30 minutes and over an hour). Scoop out the onions and carrots and keep warm. Skim the fat off the pan juices and use the rest as gravy.

8 Stir-fry the cabbage in a couple of tablespoons of cooking oil with the crushed coriander seeds and chilli flakes while someone carves the lamb for you. Mix the balsamic vinegar and torn basil leaves into the aubergine and pepper mixture.

9 Your work is done. Just serve the apple charlotte with lots of cream and get someone else to do the washing up. Burn off all the calories with a fast game of Rounders (use the bat and ball you brought for French Cricket).

L'ORANGE DANGEREUSE

you will need

2 teams and 2 oranges

aim of the game

To pass the orange from one team member to the next using only your chin and neck.

how to play

Divide into 2 teams and stand in a line. Place the orange under your chin, snuggle up to your team mate and pass the orange from your neck to theirs. They then turn and pass the orange onto the next player and so on. The winning team is the one who gets the orange passed down the line the quickest.

tip

Don't release your grip on the orange until the next player's got a good hold.

FRENCH CRICKET

This is a good afternoon game as it doesn't require everyone to play, so snoozers, snoggers and readers can head off somewhere quiet.

you will need

Bat/tennis racquet
Tennis ball

aim of the game

To be the batsman for as long as possible.

how to play

One person bats and has to fend off the ball, which is being bowled by the other players randomly. Bowlers can stand anywhere around the batsman. The bowler's aim is to hit the batsman's legs below the knees. If the bowler scores a direct strike below the knee then they become the batsman. If the batsman hits the ball they are allowed to turn to face the next bowler, if they miss the ball they can't move their feet at all so may end up trying to hit the ball while facing the opposite direction. A catch also counts as out.

THE AMBASSADORS RECEPTION

This isn't so much a game as an on-going theme for the evening. Get everyone into their fancy dress. You need to write down combinations of couples such as Thatcher and Reagan, Bonnie and Clyde, Antony and Cleopatra, Victoria and Albert, Lewinsky and Clinton etc. – the sort of people who might go to an Ambassador's Reception...

Tell all the girls who they are playing and that they have to find their partner. Don't tell them the real name, or the pseudonym, of their partner.

Give all the men one action or a phrase which is indicative of their character. Don't tell them who they're playing. For example, Reagan could be forgetful and Clinton could be smoking a cigar – but it all needs to be done subtly in the general flow of conversation. The girls have to guess from that one action or phrase who their partner is and let the men know who they are! When everyone is paired up tell them, that over the starter, they have to plan a 1-minute performance – in character – of a relevant scenario such as:

You ran over the ambassador's pooch on the way in – how do you explain it to him? or

All your ex-partners are going to be in the same room – how do you explain it to your current one?

Half the couples do one scenario, and the other half, the other.

THE ANIMAL GAME

you will need

Loud voices, good actions and quick reactions

aim of the game

To become the elephant...read on.

how to play

Sit everyone around the table Each player has to think of an animal and a noise and action for that animal. Make yourself the elephant, head of the animal kingdom, and sit at the top of the table. After everyone has demonstrated their animal's sound and action, explain to your guests that the 'animal' is the position they are sitting in not the person performing it.

The elephant then starts by standing up, doing his sound and action and then performing the routine of another animal, who in turn stands up, performs his own animal sound and action and also another animal's – and so on. This continues until there is a mistake. The person who's made the mistake then goes to the bottom of the table (on the right of the elephant) and everyone else moves up one place anti-clockwise (towards the elephant), taking on a new animal's routine. The elephant then starts a new round. The elephant can only be budged when they make a mistake. The fun really starts when everyone's moved several times and can't remember which animal's seat they're sitting in.

tips

You can't pass the 'animal' back to the previous caller.

Keep it fast and furious.

Each time someone gets the call wrong and goes to the bottom you could also give them a forfeit.

People aren't allowed to ask which animal their seat represents.

WOT A ! X BOTT

you will need

A chair
A firm hand

aim of the game

To get a good spanking!

how to play

Put everyone in a circle with the chair in the middle. Delegate one person to be a human blindfold. They sit on the chair and the person who's chosen to be spanked (we'll leave that to your imagination) hides their face in the human blindfold's lap. Everyone else takes it in turn to spank the chosen one. They have to guess whose hand is doing the spanking. If they get it right the spanker becomes the spanked and the spanked becomes a spanker.

tip

It's usually the laughter afterwards that gives away a spanker.

A ROTATIONAL DINNER PARTY

in which you can flirt all you like

A rotational dinner party is a great idea if you and some friends are single and feel you've exhausted the available talent. You're guaranteed to meet new people and, who knows, you might even like some of them. The name of the game is flirting, but if you feel you need a few ice breakers try:

round-the-table-questions

Most shaggable film star?
Best chat-up line? etc. etc.

THE EVENING WORKS LIKE THIS...

Nominate yourself as chief host(ess). This means you have to organize everything and will probably end up hosting the post-dinner party, but it does also mean that hopefully all the singletons will be pathetically grateful to you and bowled over by your organizational abilities etc., etc.

Find 3 friends of the same sex as you to host dinner parties. You all need to live pretty close to each other (maximum of 15 minutes' cab ride away). The 4 of you all invite 7 other friends, so each dinner party comprises 4 boys and 4 girls.

Allocate each house a colour: red, green, orange and yellow. As you're in charge you're red – it is the colour of lust and seduction, after all. Remember the order of the colours – it will be important. Suggest to hosts and guests that they may like to dress according to the colour of the house they're at first.

"Flirting was obviously the order of the day but Roger found himself alone with the dog..."

Make sure all the hosts have a list of each other's addresses and telephone numbers. They are going to be responsible for guests getting to the next house on the circuit. They need to work out if guests can walk to the next house or if they're going to need a taxi. Make sure all necessary taxis are booked in advance for 7.45, 8.45, 9.45 and 10.45.

Each host(ess) needs to provide pre-dinner drinks and nibbles; starter; main course and pudding. (Suggested colour-coded menus below.) Tell your 7 guests to be prompt and to bring at least 2 bottles of wine each. It's going to be a long night.

So the big night arrives... the 7 people you've invited to your house gather for drinks and nibbles at **7.00**. Elsewhere the other 3 hosts are greeting their invitees for their colour-coded nibbles. Make sure everyone is introduced and gets a chance to bat their eyelids at each other.

At **7.45** on the dot, send 4 of your guests on to the green house. Make sure they are the 4 guests who are of the opposite sex to you. At exactly the same time, the other 3 hosts must send their guests on their way, either on foot or by taxi. (This means 16 men or women are all on the move around your area at once.) So when your guests go on to the green house, the greens go on to the orange house and the oranges to the yellow. You've now got a few minutes' respite before the 4 who had drinks at the yellow house tip up at your place. Time to compare notes with the remaining gang.

Your next lot of guests should be with you at **8.00**. Serve the starter as quickly as you can. You need to get them out the door at **8.45** – they're off to try their luck at the green house and in 15 minutes you'll be able to see what the yellow house has to offer this time. So by **9.00** you should be about to serve the main course.

At **9.45** it all happens again: your lot goes off to the green house, the people who had their main course at the yellow house come to you. More talent spotting. Pudding at **10.00**.

At **10.45** everyone makes their way to your house (or to the home of whoever's hosting the post-dinner party) with all left-over booze. With all 32 of you together in the same place you can work out who's hot for who and hopefully a few romances will start to blossom... Now that's what we call a successful evening!

RED HOUSE MENU

KIR ROYALE WITH SPICY TORTILLAS CHIPS & SALSA

Put a splash of cassis in the bottom of each champagne glass (you're aiming for pink, not purple). Let your guests help themselves to chips and dip; keep those glasses topped up.

TOMATO AND MOZZARELLA SALAD WITH RED PESTO DRESSING

This can be prepared in advance and assembled at the last minute. Slice 12 beef tomatoes and 6 mozzarella balls horizontally and arrange on small plates. Make a dressing with 6 tablespoons of olive oil, 3 tablespoons of lemon juice and 3 teaspoons of tomato pesto. At the last minute give the dressing a good stir and drizzle over the salad.

CHILLI CON CARNE

Make to your favourite recipe using red chillis and lots of kidney beans. It can be made ages in advance and quickly reheated. Serve with quick-cook rice (have your trusty kettle boiled and start cooking the second your starter guests leave), sour cream, guacamole and grated cheese. Getting people to pass lots of bowls of garnishes to each other helps breaks the ice.

STRAWBERRY ICE CREAM WITH RASPBERRY SAUCE

Sieve the contents of a couple of tins of raspberries. Mix in 2 tablespoons of icing sugar and a splash of cassis. Keep in the fridge until needed. Spoon over good-quality strawberry ice cream.

GREEN HOUSE MENU

MOSCOW MULES WITH CRUDITéS AND GUACAMOLE

Make up a jug of Moscow mule: 16 shots of vodka, a good slug of lime cordial, lots of ice and top up with ginger beer. Taste (it's a tough job but someone's got to do it) and add more lime if necessary. Serve with celery and green pepper crudités and guacamole (home-made or shop bought).

SAAG BHAJI SOUP FROM MENU 8

This can be prepared well in advance. Heat the poppadums between guests.

THAI GREEN CURRY WITH GREEN BEANS

Make the Thai curry as the one in Menu 6 but substitute 8 sliced chicken breasts for the vegetables. Chop fine green beans into 5cm (2in) lengths and add when you reheat the curry between guests. Serve with noodles as they're so quick to cook.

APPLE TART FROM MENU 6

Make in advance and serve cold with thick cream.

ORANGE HOUSE MENU

HARVEY WALLBANGERS WITH CHEESY WOTSITS

Make up a jugful of the cocktail – it's basically vodka and orange juice with a good slug of grenadine. Hunt down some brightly coloured snacks in the 'kiddie crisps' section of the supermarket.

CARROT AND FENNEL SOUP FROM MENU 5

Prepare well in advance and reheat.

BAKED SALMON WITH SWEET POTATO MASH AND ORANGE PEPPER SALAD

De-seed and grill 8 orange peppers until blackened. Wrap in a plastic bag for 15 minutes then peel. Slice and dress with oil and vinegar. Put a bay leaf on top of each of 8 pieces of salmon fillet, season well then wrap individually in foil. Arrange on a baking tray. Peel, chop and boil 1kg (2¼lb) sweet potato. Drain and leave in a saucepan. This can all be done ages in advance. Heat the oven while you're eating the starter, then sling the fish in the oven as soon as you get rid of your guests. Put the pepper salad in the bottom of the oven to reheat. Warm the potato through and mash with lots of butter. Serve the fish with the foil on and let your guests unwrap it themselves.

MANGO SORBET IN BRANDY SNAP CUPS

Buy ready-made sorbet and brandy snap cups from the supermarket. Fill at the last minute. Serve on small plates.

YELLOW HOUSE MENU

PINEAPPLE FIZZ WITH CORN CHIPS AND HOUMOUS

Mix 8 shots of white rum with 1litre (1¾ pints) of pineapple juice and a bottle of champers. Lethal. Serve corn chips and houmous to absorb the alcohol.

SODA BREAD FARLS WITH MELTED CHEDDAR

Follow the recipe in Menu 9, but substitute grated cheddar for the goat's cheese. Prepare in advance and grill between guests.

STUFFED CORN-FED CHICKEN WITH POLENTA AND BABY CORN

Make up 500g (1lb 2oz) polenta according to the packet. Spread it out on a plate and allow to cool cut into wedges. Make a slit in the side of each of 8 chicken breasts (imagine it's a pitta bread). Stuff with 2 diced yellow pepper and a small herby Boursin cheese. Arrange in a roasting tin and pour over 4 glasses of white wine. Cover. At 7.45pm put the oven on to heat at 200°C/400°F/gas mark 6, put the chicken in at 8pm (while you're in the kitchen put the kettle on and heat the grill). Remove the chicken from the oven when your starter guests depart. Keep the chicken warm and use the juices in the roasting pan to make a sauce, stirring in another Boursin cheese. Grill the polenta wedges and boil 500g of baby corn.

BUTTERED BANANAS AND ICE CREAM

Follow the recipe in Menu 9. The bananas can be prepared just before your first guests arrive.

"Oh do come again..."

Acknowledgements

We couldn't have done this without the following:

Our wonderful models: **Anna, Annabelle, Andrew, Andy, Ben, Emma, Kirsten, Meg, Sarah, Simon, Sophie, Victoria, and Lucy the dog.**

Photographer **Kate Lithgow** who made them (and us) look so fantastic.

Gerry Adams from **Cornucopia** 12 Upper Tachbrook St. London SW1V 1SH (0171 828-5752) who lent us the clothes.

Sheila and Meg who got the props.

Jerry who fixed the computer in a moment of dire emergency.

Dick who shopped, ate and washed up, above and beyond the call of (husbandly) duty.

Cathy and Lulu for recipes, **Lucy and Freddie** for Cwm Llwch and **all our chums** who ate and played and commented so enthusiastically.

Absolutely **everyone at Kyle Cathie** – especially **Kyle Cathie.**

And last, but not least, wonderful **Kate Oldfield** who made it all happen.